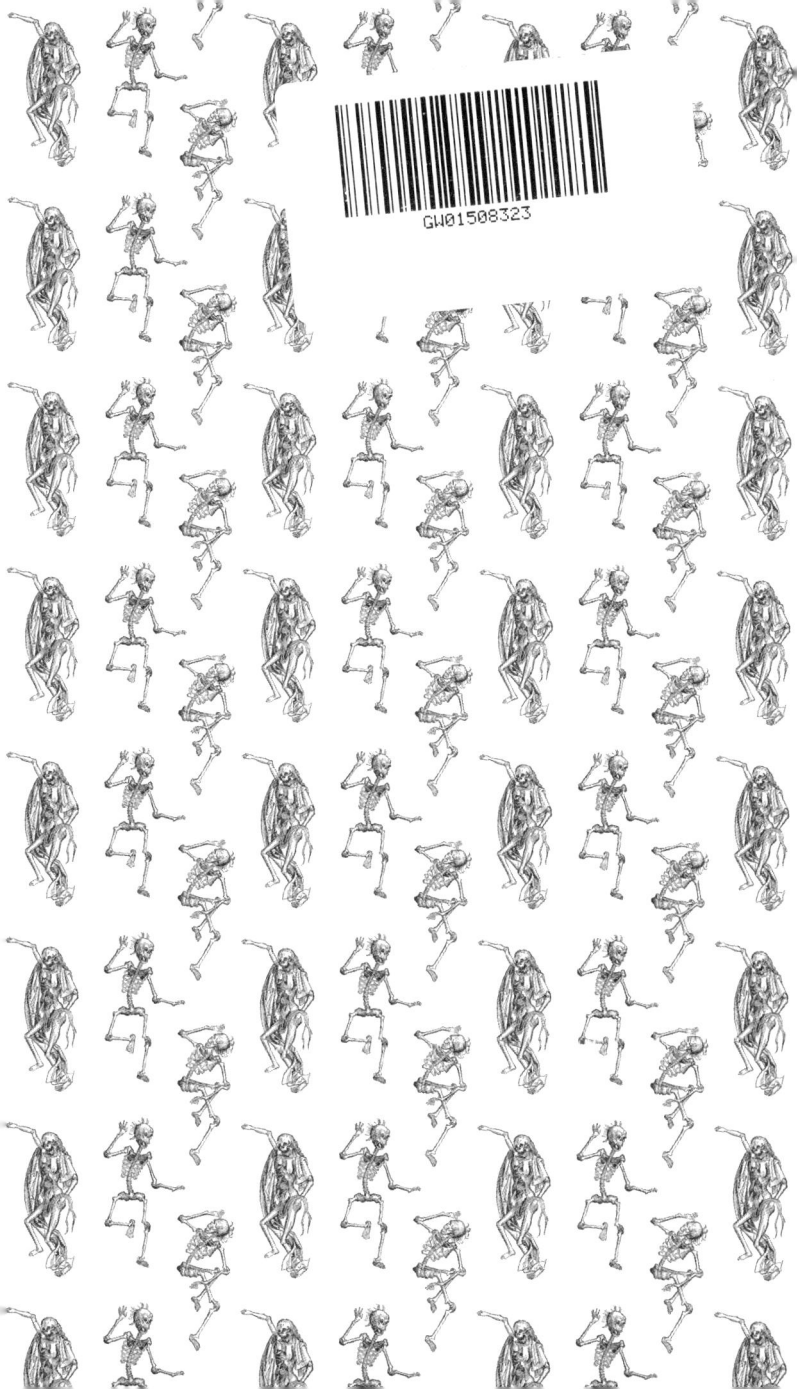

Vuckovic's
HORROR
MISCELLANY

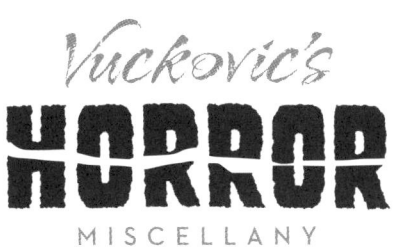

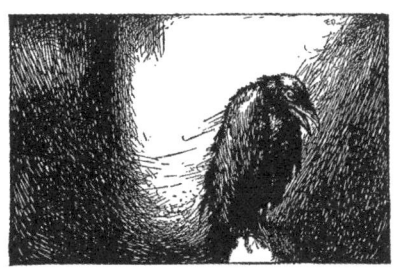

STORIES • FACTS • TALES & TRIVIA

BY JOVANKA VUCKOVIC

ILEX

VUCKOVIC'S HORROR MISCELLANY

First published in the UK, US, and Canada in 2013 by
I L E X
210 High Street
Lewes
East Sussex BN7 2NS
UK
www.ilex-press.com

Copyright © 2013 The Ilex Press Limited

PUBLISHER Alastair Campbell
CREATIVE DIRECTOR James Hollywell
MANAGING EDITOR Nick Jones
SENIOR EDITOR Ellie Wilson
COMMISSIONING EDITOR Tim Pilcher
ART DIRECTOR Julie Weir
DESIGNER Lisa McCormick
PICTURE RESEARCH Katie Greenwood
COLOR ORIGINATION Ivy Press Reprographics

Any copy of this book issued by the publisher is sold subject to the condition that it shall not by way of trade or otherwise be lent, resold, hired out, or otherwise circulated without the publisher's prior consent in any form of binding or cover other than that in which it is published and without a similar condition including these words being imposed on a subsequent purchaser.

British Library Cataloging-in-Publication Data
A catalog record for this book is available from
the British Library.

ISBN: 978-1-78157-095-1

All rights reserved. No part of this publication may be reproduced or used in any form, or by any means—graphic, electronic or mechanical, including photocopying, recording or information storage-and-retrieval systems—without the prior permission of the publisher.

Printed and bound in China

10 9 8 7 6 5 4 3 2 1

Skull icon courtesy of Jean-Benoist Prouveur
http://membres.multimania.fr/grositez/

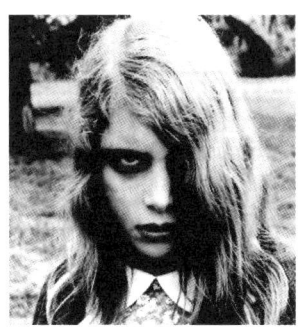

"Everybody is a book of blood;
Whenever we're opened, we're red."

CLIVE BARKER (BORN 1952)

*UK author, film director, screenwriter,
producer, actor, playwright, artist*

UNIVERSAL'S MOST MEMORABLE MONSTERS

THE PHANTOM OF THE OPERA: Born hideously deformed, Erik (Lon Chaney) is a love struck ghoul who haunts the Paris Opera House. Death: Drowned by an angry mob.

COUNT DRACULA: The Count is a financially secure Romanian expatriate vampire (Bela Lugosi) who drinks the blood of Englishwomen. Death: Staked through the heart by Abraham Van Helsing.

FRANKENSTEIN'S MONSTER: The Monster (Boris Karloff) is a collection of body parts reanimated via electricity. It mostly just wants to be loved. Death: Burned in a mill by an angry mob.

THE MUMMY: Imhotep (Boris Karloff) was an Ancient Egyptian priest who was mummified for attempting to resurrect his lover. Note to tomb-raiding archaeologists— NEVER read life-giving spells aloud near mummies! Death: Dissolved by Isis.

THE INVISIBLE MAN: Dr. Jack Griffin (Claude Rains) is a chemist who has discovered the secret of invisibility through a madness-inducing drug called monocane. Death: Shot by police.

THE WOLF MAN: Larry Talbot (Lon Chaney Jr.) is cursed with lycanthropy after he is bitten by an infected gypsy named Bela (Lugosi). Death: Bludgeoned to death by his father.

BRIDE OF FRANKENSTEIN: The Monster's Mate (Elsa Lanchester) is assembled from stolen body parts and an artificial brain. But she has no love in her undead heart for The Monster. Death: Crushed in laboratory demolition.

THE CREATURE FROM THE BLACK LAGOON: The Gill-Man (played by Ricou Browning and Ben Chapman in a suit designed by Millicent Patrick) is a piscine amphibious humanoid who just can't keep his webbed hands off the ladies. Death: Shot to death?

MR. HYDE: The hairy, dentally challenged, homicidal side of Dr. Jekyll (Fredric March), a mild mannered scientist whose research is rooted in the duality of human nature. Death: Shot by police.

THE HUNCHBACK OF NOTRE DAME: Quasimodo (Lon Chaney) is a deformed bell-ringer living in Paris' Notre Dame Cathedral. Deaf and half-blind, he'll never win the affections of Esmerelda. Death: Stabbed in the back.

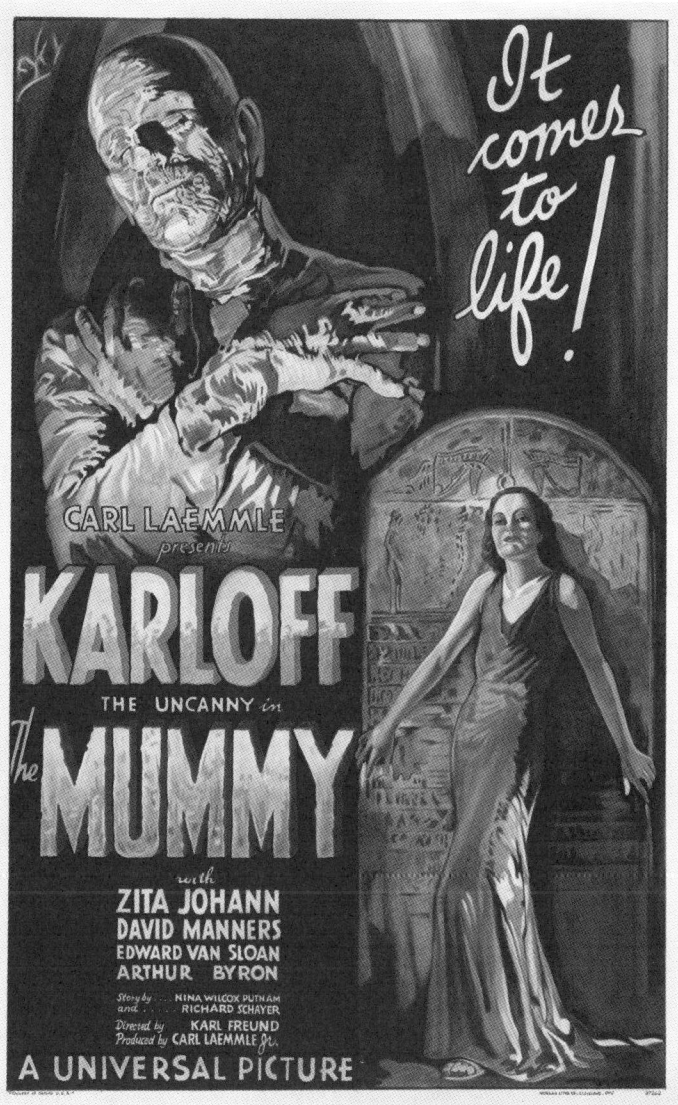

> *"There is a fifth dimension, beyond that which is known to man.
> It is a dimension as vast as space and as timeless as infinity.
> It is the middle ground between light and shadow, between science
> and superstition, and it lies between the pit of man's fears and the
> summit of his knowledge. This is the dimension of imagination.
> It is an area which we call the Twilight Zone."*
> ROD SERLING (1924-1975), The Twilight Zone

M

DIRECTOR FRITZ LANG'S FIRST "TALKIE," *M* is largely considered the progenitor to films such as *Psycho* (1960), *The Silence of the Lambs* (1991), and *Se7en* (1995). This 1931 drama—originally called *The Murderers Are Among Us*—stars Peter Lorre in a benchmark performance as Hans Beckert, a deranged serial killer and rapist who is terrorizing a German town. When the police fail to apprehend him, other criminals join the manhunt. Although Lang denied it, Beckert is allegedly based on the real life killer Peter Kürten (AKA the "Vampire of Düsseldorf"), whom the Berlin police had difficulty catching in the 1920s. It is also one of the first films to use a musical leitmotif to signify a character; Beckert whistles *In the Hall of the Mountain King* from Edvard Grieg's *Peer Gynt Suite No.1*.

FIVE FAMOUS GRAVEYARD POEMS

A Night-Piece on Death
THOMAS PARNELL (1721)

The Complaint, or Night Thoughts on Life, Death, and Immortality
EDWARD YOUNG (1742–45)

The Grave ROBERT BLAIR (1743)

The Pleasures of Melancholy
THOMAS WARTON (1747)

Elegy Written in a Country Churchyard THOMAS GRAY (1750)

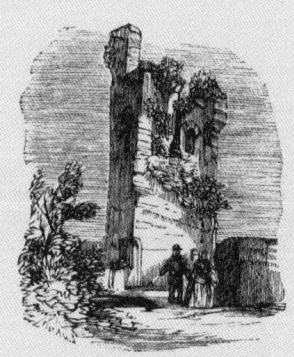

EC COMICS

First known as "educational comics," EC Comics was transformed in 1947, when William Gaines took over his father's company. Rebranded "Entertaining Comics," the imprint dispensed with American history and Bible stories and began printing fiction in the genres of romance, crime, westerns, and eventually . . . horror.

In 1950, Gaines took two of the company's existing titles, *Crime Patrol* and *War Against Crime*, and re-launched them as *Crypt of Terror* (later renamed, *Tales from the Crypt*) and *Vault of Horror*. The horror titles proved popular and with the help of intrepid editors/illustrators Al Feldstein and Harvey Kurtzman, more followed. *The Haunt of Fear* and *Shock SuspenStories* featured astonishing artwork by freelancers Jack Davis, Frank Frazetta, Graham Ingels, Basil Wolverton, Johnny Craig, and Reed Crandall. These artists were given unprecedented freedom to illustrate the gleefully nasty stories, which featured plenty of violence and gore as ironic fates were meted out to protagonists in gruesome poetic justice. A trio of glib horror hosts—The Crypt Keeper, The Vault Keeper, and The Old Witch—introduced the stories, threw jabs at each other, and spoke directly to readers. The kids ate it up.

But the romance didn't last long, however. When Dr. Fredric Wertham's infamous *The Seduction of the Innocent: The Influence of Comic Books on Today's Youth* saw print, it exerted its own influence on parents and helped usher in the regulatory Comics Code Authority. The CCA instated a "Comics Code" in 1954 that effectively killed horror comics altogether on September 14, 1954. "Horror" and "Terror" were banned from use in titles, and practically every monster—from zombies to werewolves—was verboten subject matter— as was the use of any "gruesome illustrations." As Gaines said, in the nationally televised court case: "It would be just as difficult to explain the harmless thrill of a horror story to a Dr. Wertham, as it would be to explain the sublimeness of love to a frigid old maid." A similar ban occurred in the UK with Parliament passing *The Children and Young Persons (Harmful Publications) Act* on June 6, 1955—making it illegal to print, publish, or sell horror comics.

EC managed to stay afloat on the success of its sole Code-proof satire publication, *MAD* magazine but the EC horror comic stayed in the ground. It resurfaced 20 years later when British horror film production company Amicus released a film version of *Tales from the Crypt* (1972) and *The Vault of Horror* followed a year later.

Other notable EC Comics-inspired anthologies include the exceptional George Romero/Stephen King collaboration *Creepshow* (1982), its sequel *Creepshow 2* (1987), the *Tales from the Crypt* television series (1989-1996), *Tales from the Cryptkeeper* (1993), *Secrets of the Cryptkeeper's Haunted House* (1997), *Demon Knight* (1995), *Bordello of Blood* (1996), and *Ritual* (2000).

ATTACK OF THE FIFTIES' "B" MOVIE!

WORLD WAR II WAS OVER. 40 million people were dead. The silliness of *Abbott & Costello Meet Frankenstein* put a stop to the Universal monster movies, which could no longer capture the zeitgeist of post-War America anyway. People lived with the fear of Cold War, furry-faced monsters weren't cutting it, and new breed of monster came onto the scene: Technology. The Atom Bomb. America was dealing with the guilt of dropping one on another nation and the fear of potential retaliation and the apocalyptic aftermath. People were watching the skies, and they thought they saw something fall from it in 1947 at Roswell.

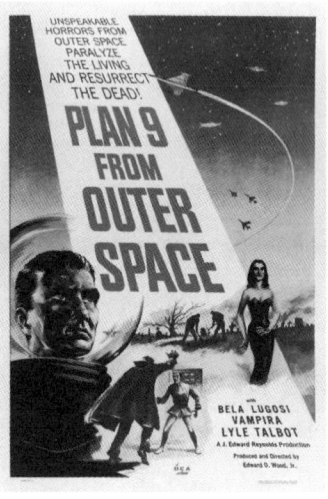

All of this had an enormous impact on the public consciousness, which was forever changed between 1940 and 1950. As such, the horror films of the 1950s are rooted in fear of science, technology, and the speed at which they were advancing. Hollywood was too busy trying to keep up with its own technological advances to put much effort into horror films. But the demand from teenagers (accessed via the new medium of television advertising) at drive-ins gave rise to the quick and cheap Hollywood "B" movie. Mutated monsters (*Godzilla*, 1954), killer bugs (*Them!* 1954), oversized babes (*Attack of the 50 Foot Woman*, 1958), and alien invaders (*It Came from Outer Space*, 1953) ran rampant. Mind control and paranoia were the order of the day throughout the 1950s—in both the ludicrous B movies (*Plan 9 From Outer Space*, 1959) and more serious offerings (*Invasion of the Body Snatchers*, 1956).

1953's *The Beast from 20,000 Fathoms* was the highest grossing film of the year, raking in $5 million (production budget was a mere $210,000). Based on a Ray Bradbury short, *The Beast . . .* had everything the American public needed in a film: a big, bad, irradiated, carnivorous dinosaur from the ocean depths that gets defeated by "good radiation." *The Beast*'s . . . cinematic success encouraged the production of many more "creature features," and was a huge influence on Japan's own mutated sea monster movie, *Godzilla*—released the following year, in 1954.

> *"Monsters in movies are us, always us, one way or the other. They're us with hats on. The zombies in George Romero's movies are us. They're hungry. Monsters are us, the dangerous parts of us. The part that wants to destroy. The part of us with the reptile brain. The part of us that's vicious and cruel. We express these in our stories as these monsters out there."*
>
> JOHN CARPENTER (BORN 1948)
> *US director, screenwriter, producer, and composer*

THE WALKING DEAD

ZOMBIES HAVE BEEN LUMBERING around the genre since the 1930s. They breached the mainstream when they moonwalked into living rooms via Michael Jackson's *Thriller* (1982), and again with the popular first person shooter *Resident Evil* video game series (1996), but no one could have anticipated the global fandemic of *The Walking Dead*.

First published by Image Comics in 2003, the post-apocalyptic story centers on police officer Rick Grimes, who awakes from a coma, weeks after a zombie outbreak has devastated the population. Reunited with his wife and son, Rick mostly struggles to endure encounters with other survivors, who often pose a bigger threat to him and his family than the flesh-hungry "roamers." To bolster this point, and also to make a nod to George Romero's *Night of the Living Dead*, the book is presented entirely in black and white.

Series creator Robert Kirkman pays further homage to Romero in his characterizations and slow, lumbering zombies. You won't find a running corpse anywhere in his books. The series—currently drawn by Charlie Adlard and Cliff Rathburn, recently surpassed 100 issues with no end in sight—was picked up by AMC and began airing on US TV on Halloween 2010, with Frank Darabont executive producing. The show was a massive hit. Three seasons later, *The Walking Dead* has become the most-watched basic cable drama telecast in history. Remarkably, the show features some of the goriest and best zombie make-up effects ever seen on television, courtesy Greg Nicotero and KNB EFX.

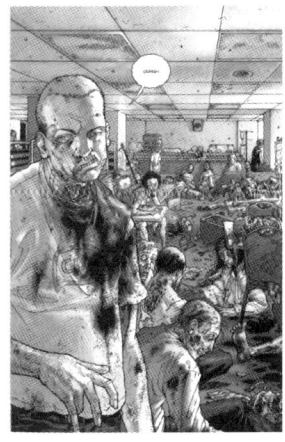

THE MODERN PROMETHEUS

LARGELY CONSIDERED TO BE THE progenitor of the science fiction genre, Mary Shelley's *Frankenstein* is also perhaps the most pervasive cultural myth ever written. In it, an unorthodox scientist named Victor Frankenstein gives life to a monstrous abomination of corporeal indestructibility that runs afoul of its creator, leaving a trail of murder and mayhem all the way to the Arctic Circle. It is told via a correspondence of letters by Captain Robert Walton, who encounters Frankenstein (and later, his notorious Monster) on an arctic expedition.

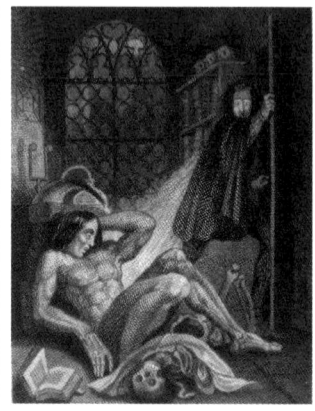

Frankenstein was first published anonymously in 1818, when Shelley was just 21 years old, to a receptive audience. A second edition, which attributed the name of its female author, garnered nasty reviews from sexist critics seeking to demolish the work. By 1823 there were at least five stage plays in London, England. Shelley herself attended and enjoyed one of them—*Presumption: or, The Fate of Frankenstein*. It wasn't long before Shelley's "Monster" began appearing in crossovers, under the misnomer "Frankenstein." An 1826 production entitled *The Devil among the Players* featured Frankenstein, The Vampyre (from John Polidori's short story), and Faust, all appearing together for the first time.

Later editions of *Frankenstein* include an 1831 volume that was heavily rewritten by Shelley in an attempt to make the story more conservative, but the 1818 edition remains the definitive work. Today, Frankenstein's monster has appropriated the name of its creator and is part of the cultural consciousness. Most children are aware of Frankenstein by the age of two—as it appears in cartoons, cereal boxes, and cadres of cultural novelties. An indispensible metaphor about man's desire for forbidden knowledge, that creativity is dangerous without moral responsibility.

"I delight in what I fear."
SHIRLEY JACKSON (1916-1965), *US author*

A GOTHIC HORROR READER: THE FIRST WAVE

THE CASTLE OF OTRANTO—Horace Walpole (1764)

THE OLD ENGLISH BARON—Clara Reeve (1778)

HISTORY OF THE CALIPH VATHEK—William Thomas Beckford (1786)

JUSTINE—Marquis de Sade (1791)

THE MYSTERIES OF UDOLPHO—Ann Radcliffe (1794)

THE NECROMANCER—Carl Friedrich Kahlert (1794)

THE MONK—Matthew Gregory Lewis (1796)

THE ITALIAN—Ann Radcliffe (1797)

FRANKENSTEIN, OR, THE MODERN PROMETHEUS—Mary Shelley (1818)

THE VAMPYRE—John William Polidori (1819)

MELMOTH THE WANDERER—Charles Robert Maturin (1820)

SALATHIEL THE IMMORTAL—George Croly (1829)

THE HUNCHBACK OF NOTRE DAME—Victor Hugo (1831)

THE FALL OF THE HOUSE OF USHER—Edgar Allan Poe (1839)

MARY SHELLEY

MARY SHELLEY (NÉE MARY WOLLSTONECRAFT GODWIN) was born on August 30, 1797 to political philosopher William Godwin and feminist writer Mary Wollstonecraft. Her mother died when she was just 11 days old. At just 17 years old, she began having an affair with one of her father's political followers, Percy Bysshe Shelley, a married man. Percy abandoned his then-pregnant wife Harriet—who later committed suicide—before running off with Mary and her stepsister, Claire, to Europe. They married in late 1816, the same year Mary conceived of the idea for her debut novel *Frankenstein*. They spent much of their time dodging creditors and public outcry regarding Percy's desertion of his first wife and child. The Shelleys had four children, three of which died as infants, which left Mary in a deep depression. Beset by financial problems they fled England for Italy. Their fourth and only surviving child Percy Florence Shelley was born in Florence on November 12, 1819. Her husband drowned when his sailboat sank during a storm in the Bay of La Spezia. Mary returned to England following the tragedy and died of a suspected brain tumor at the age of 53.

SEMANTICS

hor·ror noun (plural horrors)
1 an intense feeling of fear, shock, or disgust.
2 a thing causing such a feeling.
3 intense dismay.
4 *informal* a bad or mischievous person, especially a child.

Oxford English Dictionary

I AM LEGEND

"I DIDN'T COME UP WITH the idea for *Night of the Living Dead*, I stole it from Richard Matheson," director George Romero has often said, referring to Matheson's seminal 1954 vampire tale, *I Am Legend*—one of the most important novels in the progression of horror cinema.

The story revolves around Robert Neville, the sole survivor of a devastating pandemic plague that has turned the population into bloodthirsty vampires. Neville spends his days outside scavenging and staking vampires in Los Angeles. By night he is barricaded indoors and taunted by his turned neighbors and friends. It is implied that the contagion was transmitted by a surge in the mosquito population, following a war. For whatever reason, Neville is immune and he desperately wants to find a cure. His only friend is a dog that he crushingly has to put down after it is infected. Neville ends up becoming so proficient in killing vampires, that his nightly visitors greatly diminish until one day he spots a female survivor out in the daylight and takes her in. But is Ruth who she says she is? To say more would be spoiling one of the most heart-breaking endings ever to grace the printed page.

With *I Am Legend*, Matheson introduced the germ theory of vampirism, an idea that has had a tremendous influence on the zombie film subgenre. Up to this point, vampires were created via the supernatural means. The tale was adapted for screen in 1964 as *The Last Man on Earth*, starring Vincent Price as Robert Neville. This film had an enormous impact on filmmaker George Romero, who openly cribbed from it and *I Am Legend* to conceive of his iconic apocalyptic zombie siege film, *Night of the Living Dead* (1968). The film adaptations have demonstrated the law of diminishing returns with 1971's *Omega Man,* and 2007's *I Am Legend*, starring Will Smith. The latter is a risible, inexcusable example of Hollywood's inability to recognize a masterful story when it sees one. *I Am Legend* still awaits a faithful cinematic adaptation, but the original text is practically timeless and compulsory reading.

WAR OF THE WORLDS RADIO BROADCAST

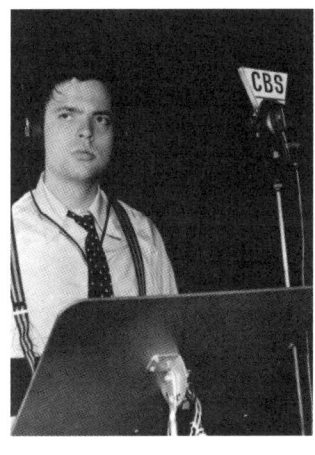

ON SUNDAY OCTOBER 30, 1938, millions of WABC listeners were locked into a series of radio bulletins delivering news about the arrival of Martians on planet Earth. Believing an actual invasion was currently in progress, people fled their homes and tried to escape the invasion in their vehicles. What they were hearing, though, was merely an adaptation of H. G. Wells' well-known novel, *War of the Worlds* (1898), narrated by dramatist and future filmmaker Orson Welles. A young theatre troupe, led by Welles, put together the broadcast with the highest level of verisimilitude on radio to date. The story was re-written and set in modern day New Jersey, intense sound effects were added to "real time" interviews and musical numbers were interrupted by news bulletins—bolstering the illusion that the entire broadcast was real, especially for listeners who were tuning in late. Though there were several notices throughout the broadcast indicating it was merely a radio play, thousands of listeners panicked and were subsequently outraged at Welles, who had in one fell swoop, galvanized his career as a storyteller.

THE TRIAL

IMAGINE BEING ARRESTED, tried, and punished for an undisclosed crime that requires no evidence to prove your guilt. Such is the uniquely cerebral and atmospheric horror of Franz Kafka's *The Trial* (1925). Josef K. wakes one morning to find himself inexplicably arrested by an immense and ubiquitous judicial organization that threatens to destroy him through isolation and madness. Although not typically included in a timeline of horror, Kafka's oppressive, waking nightmare has had a strong influence on modern horror fiction, including the work of Ramsey Campbell and Dennis Etchison. The unfinished novel was released against (the deceased) Kafka's will. It did, however, include a chapter that features the terrible death of the novel's protagonist. Few stories are this crushing and nihilistic. In 1962 Orson Welles adapted a strong film version.

KING KONG

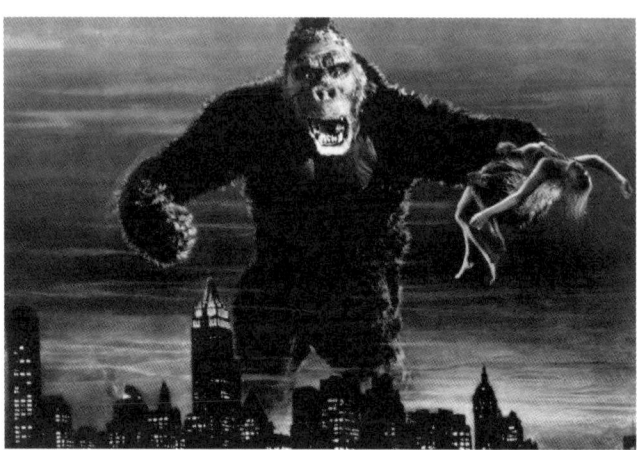

HANDS DOWN ONE OF THE BEST monster movies ever made, *King Kong* (1933) is a spectacular feat of the imagination and a stop-motion masterpiece. Director Merian C. Cooper was already famous for filming exotic wildlife documentaries when he conceived the idea for the giant prehistoric ape, Kong. Cooper originally wanted to capture a real ape from the Congo but after witnessing the stop-motion effects of animator Willis H. O'Brien (*The Lost World*, 1925), he and producer Ernest B. Schoedsack had a change of heart.

Led by Ace filmmaker Carl Denham (Robert Armstrong), a film crew travels aboard the Venture to Skull Island where they encounter an 18-foot prehistoric ape (publicity materials would advertise 60 feet), who takes a shine to their female passenger, unemployed actress Ann Darrow (Fay Wray). Ann is kidnapped by the island natives and offered as a sacrifice to the godlike beast, then rescued by the ship's mate Jack Driscoll (Bruce Cabot). But Denham traps Kong with the intention of bringing him back to New York and show case him as "The Eighth Wonder of the World." Big mistake.

Packed with action, adventure, mystery, and horror, *King Kong* is arguably the most important adventure film in cinema history, worth the price of admission for the monster fights alone. While protecting Ann, Kong spectacularly defeats a Stegosaurus, a Pteranodon, a Tyrannosaurus Rex (in a violent, pre-Code scene) and a Plesiosaurus. *Kong*'s shadow looms large over the work of Ray Harryhausen (*Jason and the Argonauts*, 1963), Ishirō Honda (*Godzilla*, 1954), hundreds of creature features of the 1950s, George Lucas' *Star Wars* (1977) as well as contemporary colossal creature epics such as *Jurassic Park* (1993), and *Cloverfield* (2008).

GODZILLA

Tokyo, 1954. With the wounds of the atomic bombings of Hiroshima and Nagasaki still fresh in the public consciousness, the Japanese film studio Toho conceived of a monster that embodied the very real terror of nuclear detonation. They called it Gojira, a portmanteau of two words, gorira ("gorilla") and kujira ("whale"). Gojira is a giant aquatic, bipedal dinosaur whose mutations are presumed to be a result of nuclear weapons testing irradiation. In the film, Gojira (known in North America as Godzilla) rises from the depths of the sea screeching a (copyrighted) mechanical roar and obliterates the city with its atomic breath. Through the ensuing tidal wave of sequels and crossovers, Godzilla has been reduced to silliness, but in its original incarnation the monster is downright menacing. Images of Japanese people burning alive from Godzilla's death ray hauntingly recall the devastation of the A-bomb. *Gojira* turned out to be much more than a remake of *The Beast From 20,000 Fathoms*, it is an intelligent allegory and precautionary tale from Japan's point of view. It set the standard for all kaiju (giant monster) films that would follow, all the way up to, and including, Guillermo del Toro's *Pacific Rim* (2013). An inferior American version was released in 1956, starring Raymond Burr as a reporter. It unwisely edits out much of the thoughtful anti-nuclear sentiment of the *Gojira*, which is, after all, the spiny backbone of the monster.

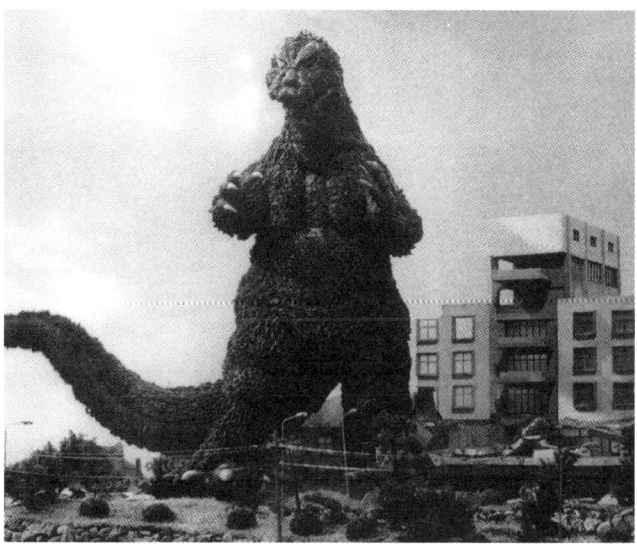

PAUL NASCHY

NICKNAMED THE SPANISH LON CHANEY, Paul Naschy (real name Jacinto Molina Álvarez) was an incredibly prolific actor, writer, director, and championship weightlifter who made well over one hundred feature films in Spain. He was a true horror legend and champion of fantastic cinema, having portrayed innumerable characters including Jack the Ripper, Fu Manchu, Frankenstein, The Wolfman, Count Dracula, The Hunchback, and The Mummy. He is most well known for creating the character of Waldemar Daninsky, a Polish werewolf Naschy played in 12 films beginning with 1968's *La Marca del Hombre Lobo*. His autobiography, *Memoirs of a Wolfman*, was published in 2009, and a documentary entitled *The Man Who Saw Frankenstein Cry* was completed the following year, hosted by Mick Garris (*Masters of Horror*, *The Shining*).

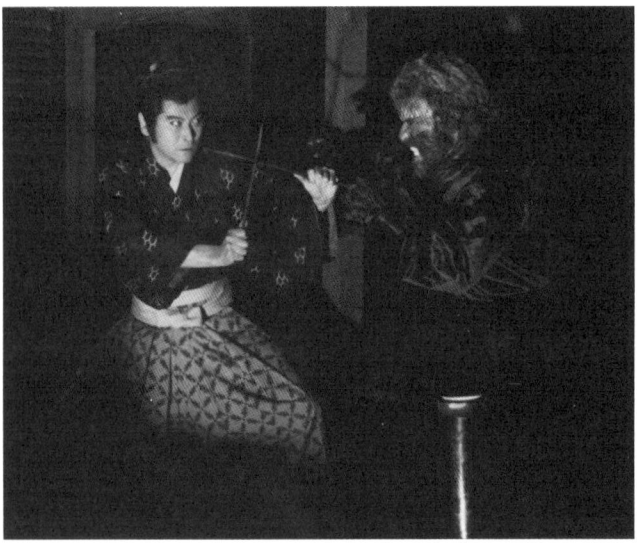

> "Frightening people is something that you have to think about —you can't just allow it to happen."
> VINCENT PRICE (1911-1993), *US actor*

EDOGAWA RAMPO

SAY HIS NAME FIVE TIMES FAST. Sound familiar? Edogawa Rampo is the *nom de plume* of Tarō Hirai (1894-1965), a Japanese detective mystery writer who adored Edgar Allan Poe so much that the he derived a punning phonemic approximation based on his name. Western mystery authors such as Sir Arthur Conan Doyle and Maurice Leblanc heavily influenced Rampo, but it was Poe's tales of the macabre that most inspired him to become Japan's first modern mystery writer.

In his early career Rampo developed Poe's material to fit into Japanese culture, but ended up leaning towards "ero gero" (erotic grotesque) subject matter. The result was a beautifully strange, perverse vision of gothic horror all his own. Ten of his more horrific short stories from this period were translated into English in 1956 and published under the title, *Japanese Tales of Mystery and Imagination*. Some of them border on the bizarre. In *The Human Chair*, for example, a man buries himself in a chair so that he can feel the "loves" of the women who sit on top of him. *The Hell of Mirrors* is a tale of technology out of control in which a deranged young voyeur traps himself inside a giant ball he has fashioned from mirrors so that he can enjoy its hidden pleasures. *The Caterpillar* is a horrifying tale about a quadriplegic, deaf, mute, war veteran (described as a "lump of flesh with eyes") whose wife plucks out what remains of his humanity.

During the 1930s the Japanese government forbade topics of "horror dementia, bizarre behavior, cult religions, drugs, and sadism" as morally deviant. *The Caterpillar* was banned and Rampo was forced to tone down his output. He's best known in Japan for his Hardy Boys-style *Boys Detective Gang* series, but he's most remembered in America for his erotic grotesque brand of horror fiction.

COUNT CHOCULA

GENERAL MILLS' dark prince of insulin spikes, Count Chocula, is the fanged face of the eponymous monster-themed breakfast cereal. The cartoon vampire who prefers the taste of chocolate to blood is based on Bram Stoker's Count Dracula and made his supermarket debut in March, 1971. Since then the "super sweet monster with the super sweet cereal" has starred in many memorable television commercials, croaking the tagline, "I vant to eat your cereal!" in a Bela Lugosi-style voice. The popular cereal is sold seasonally around Halloween. Other Mills monster-themed breakfast cereals include Franken Berry, Boo Berry, Fruit Brute, and Fruity Yummy Mummy. How about a monster for breakfast today?

VINCENT PRICE

Where would the horror genre be without Vincent Price? A man whose legacy of horror includes dozens of stage shows, 45 horror films, scores of television performances, and thousands of radio appearances. The theatre-trained actor had already established a successful career in film before he made his first foray into horror with the Boris Karloff/Basil Rathbone film, *Tower of London,* in 1939. Next was *The Invisible Man Returns* (1940), a sequel to the Universal adaptation of H.G. Wells' famous story (originally starring Claude Rains). But it was 1950's *The House of Wax* that cemented Price as a master of the macabre. It was a turning point for the actor, who was struggling with the decision to remain in the movies or return to the theatre. He made the right decision, because *House of Wax* was a financial and critical success, the first 3-D film to make the box office top 10.

Price perfected what he affectionately called his "sinister image" in subsequent genre films, *The Mad Magician* (1954), *The Fly* (1958), *Return of the Fly* (1959), and the William Castle thriller, *The Tingler* (1959). By now filmgoers were accustomed to Price's hammy grandstanding and sinister laugh. After all, most of the horror films of the 1950s weren't taking themselves too seriously. All that changed with the turnover of the decade and Price's regular appearances in Roger Corman's Edgar Allan Poe adaptations.

Largely considered Corman's finest achievements, the Poe adaptations cinematic value far exceeded their low budgets. Teaming up with writer Richard Matheson, Corman delivered eight films adapted from Poe's work: *House of Usher* (1960), *The Pit and the Pendulum* (1961), *Tales of Terror* (1962), *The Comedy of Terrors* (1963), *The Raven* (1963), *The Masque of the Red Death* (1964), and *The Tomb of Ligeia* (1965). Price starred in all of them except *The Premature Burial* (1962).

Price also starred in *The Last Man on Earth* (1964), the first adaptation of Matheson's seminal vampire story, *I Am Legend*. He played the titular masked musician of *The Abominable Dr. Phibes* twice; took a turn as the particularly nasty witch hunter, Matthew Hopkins, in *Witchfinder General* (1968); and an actor taking creative revenge on his critics in *Theatre of Blood* (1973). He also played Egghead in the *Batman* Sixties' television series; was the host of the Canadian children's show *The Hilarious House of Frightenstein*; played Edward Scissorhands' genial inventor; and the creepy narrator of Michael Jackson's *Thriller*. In his personal life, Price was a gourmand and art collector who published books on both subjects and always took the time to correspond with his fans. He died of lung cancer on October 25, 1993 at the age of 82.

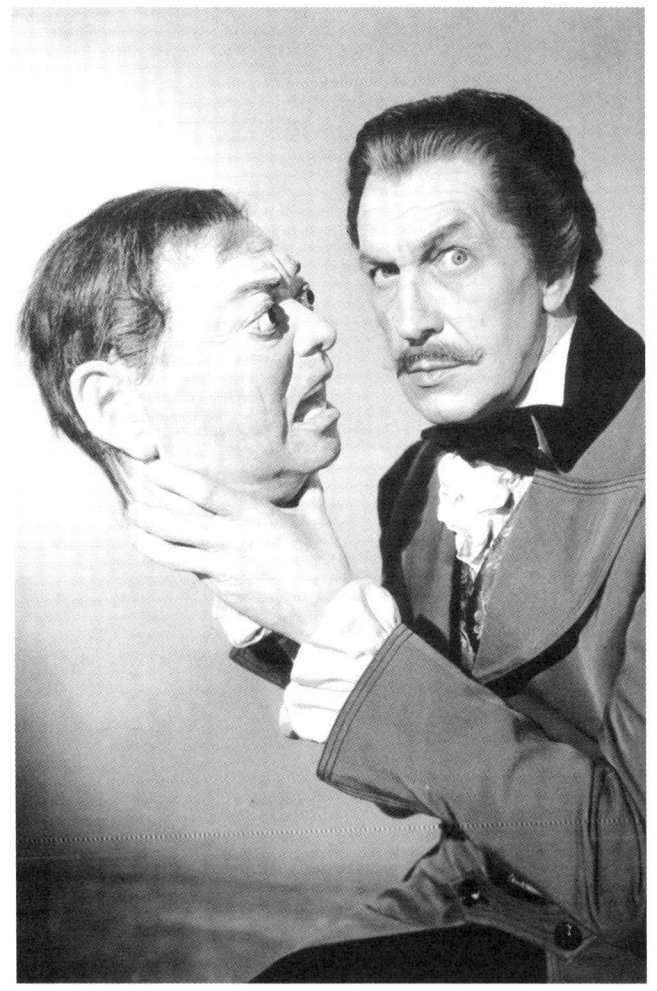

TOP 13 VAMPIRE FILMS

1. NOSFERATU (dir. F.W. Murnau, 1922)
2. DEATHDREAM/DEAD OF NIGHT (dir. Bob Clark, 1972)
3. CRONOS (dir. Guillermo del Toro, 1993)
4. LET'S SCARE JESSICA TO DEATH (dir. John D. Hancock, 1971)
5. NEAR DARK (dir. Kathryn Bigelow, 1987)
6. MARTIN (dir. George A. Romero, 1976)
7. LET THE RIGHT ONE IN (dir. Tomas Alfredson, 2008)
8. SALEM'S LOT (dir. Tobe Hooper, 1979)
9. SHADOW OF THE VAMPIRE (dir. E. Elias Merhige, 2000)
10. VAMPYR (dir. Carl Theodor Dreyer, 1932)
11. HORROR OF DRACULA (dir. Terence Fisher, 1958)
12. RABID (dir. David Cronenberg, 1977)
13. BRAM STOKER'S DRACULA (dir. Francis Ford Coppola, 1992)

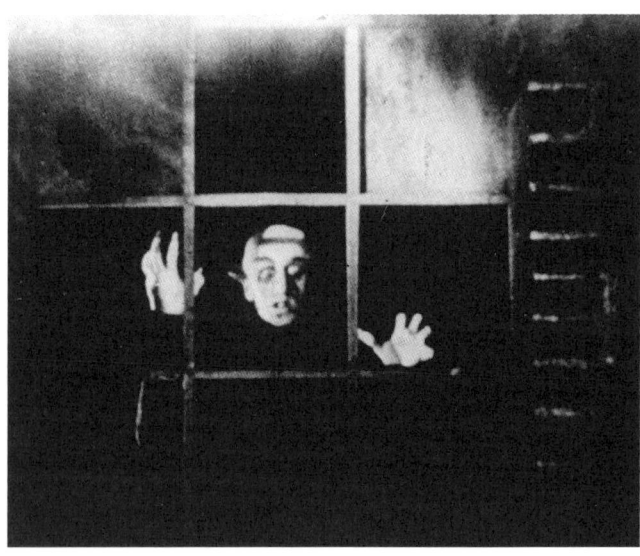

BLACK SABBATH

Named after the 1963 Mario Bava film starring Boris Karloff, Black Sabbath are an English rock band whose lyrics often feature supernatural, occult, and horror-themed imagery. Formed in 1969, Black Sabbath's dark aesthetic was combined with tuned-down unison guitar playing and the overall effect was a dense, gloomy, unsettling sound unlike anything else that had come out of the late-1960s.

The band's first record *Black Sabbath* (1970) featured singer Ozzy Osbourne screeching out dreary songs such as *Evil Woman* (a cover of a blues rock song), the lilting, doom-laden self-titled track, *NIB* (written from the point of view of Lucifer), and the H.P. Lovecraft-inspired, *Behind the Wall of Sleep*. The inner gatefold sleeve of the original release even featured an inverted cross with a poem inside it—fuelling suspicion that the band's members were Occultists and Satan worshippers. The black magic wasn't without its charms, because within just a few months the band was recording its next studio album, the magnum opus *Paranoid*. 16 albums followed, with various line-up changes—most famously with Osbourne being fired and replaced by Ronnie James Dio in 1979, and again in 1982, when Dio left and was replaced by Deep Purple's Ian Gillan.

Despite a revolving door of vocalists that eventually led back to Ozzy, Black Sabbath has sustained its dark appeal and is credited as the progenitor of the "heavy metal," "stoner rock," and "doom metal" genres as well as the first band to embrace the horror aesthetic. They have sold over 70 million records worldwide.

THE GREAT GOD PAN

A ruthless scientist desperate to rend the veil of reality performs an operation on the brain of a young girl. He believes the surgery will allow her to see the true god of nature (sort of like the sunglasses do in John Carpenter's *They Live*, but much more dangerous). Of course the truth is too shocking for the human mind and the young girl is driven to madness and death but not before giving birth to Helen Vaughn, a beautiful seductress who inspires madness and suicide in the men she meets decades later. Helen is the monstrous half human offspring of Pan and the protean Femme Fatale of many future horror films. Arthur Machen's 1894 novella was a massive influence on the cosmic horror of H.P. Lovecraft, who paid homage to it in the short story *The Dunwich Horror* (1928). Occultist Aleister Crowley was a huge fan of Machen's mystic writing, but the Welsh author detested "The Great Beast" in return.

10 MUST-SEE FIFTIES HORROR FILMS

1. THE DAY THE EARTH STOOD STILL (dir. Robert Wise, 1951)
2. THE THING FROM ANOTHER WORLD (dir. Christian Nyby, 1951)
3. THE BEAST FROM 20,000 FATHOMS (dir. Eugene Lourie, 1953)
4. HOUSE OF WAX (dir. André de Toth, 1953)
5. THE WAR OF THE WORLDS (dir. Byron Haskin, 1953)
6. CREATURE FROM THE BLACK LAGOON (dir. Jack Arnold, 1954)
7. THEM! (dir. Gordon M. Douglas, 1954)
8. THE FLY (dir. Kurt Neumann, 1958)
9. THE BLOB (dir. Irvin Shortess Yeaworth, Jr. 1958)
10. INVASION OF THE BODY SNATCHERS (dir. Don Siegel, 1956)

RAY BRADBURY

RAY DOUGLAS BRADBURY WAS BORN on August 22, 1920 in Waukegan, Illinois. He wrote his earliest stories in 1931 on butcher paper and ended his formal education after graduating from the Los Angeles high school in 1938. He spent his post secondary school days selling newspapers on street corners of Los Angeles and his nights at the library, behind a rented typewriter. He contributed to fan magazines and even started one of his own in 1939; *Futuria Fantasia* lasted just four issues but was funded by *Famous Monsters* magazine editor, Forrest J Ackerman. Bradbury's first paying gig was a short story called *Pendulum*, for *Super Science Stories* (1941). He quit selling newspapers to become a professional writer in 1943. By 1947 he had his first collection of macabre and lyrical short stories published by Arkham House entitled, *Dark Carnival*. A self-described "quasi god-son of Edgar Allan Poe," his stories reflected an obsession with aging, death, and the nostalgic desire to maintain contact with his inner child. He would go on to achieve international fame with the publication of monumental fiction landmarks such as *The Martain Chronicles* (1950), *The Illustrated Man* (1951), *Farenheit 451* (1953), and *Something Wicked This Way Comes* (1962). Today Bradbury is so beloved he has earned a star on the Hollywood Walk of Fame (6644 Hollywood Blvd), an asteroid was named in his honor ("9766 Bradbury") and a moon crater ("Dandelion Crater") was named after his story *Dandelion Wine*. He died on June 5, 2012 after a long illness.

GRIMM'S FAIRY TALES

SEX, MURDER, CANNIBALISM, MUTILATION, INFANTICIDE, incest, brutality, and violence: this is the stuff of good German fairy tales. *Children's and Household Tales* (*Kinder und Hausmärchen*) is a collection of capricious and cruel Germanic folk tales adapted from the oral tradition by brothers Jacob and Wilhelm Grimm. Originally published in 1812, the first edition collected 86 didactic stories that were initially criticized as being wholly inappropriate children (courtesy the aforementioned atrocities). Later editions varnished the tales with sweetness, excised sexual references (such as Rapunzel naively asking why her dress is getting tight around her belly) but largely retained the violence native to these stories, especially when it came to revenge. Famous characters from Brothers Grimm include Rumpelstiltskin, Rapunzel, Cinderella, Sleeping Beauty, Little Red Riding Hood, Hansel and Gretel and Snow White. But in Grimm's original version of *Snow White*, her cruel mother (later changed into a step-mother) is forced to dance to death in a pair of red-hot iron shoes her daughter's wedding. In *The Sleeping Beauty*, the lovely princess is raped by the King while sleeping and she awakes to find herself the mother of two children. And in *The Frog Prince*, the princess throws the frog against a wall instead of kissing it.

COUNTESS ELIZABETH BÁTHORY

ERZSÉBET (AKA ELIZABETH) Báthory de Ecsed (1560-1614) was a Hungarian countess and psychopathic sadist who, along with four accomplices, attained notoriety by torturing and killing hundreds of people in her castle between 1585 and 1610. Báthory's true body count is unknown, but is speculated to be as high as 650, making her the most prolific female serial killer in history. She came to be known as the "Blood Countess" and "The Bloody Lady of Čachtice." She is said to have murdered the children, all girls, and bathed in their blood in a ritualistic attempt at everlasting beauty. This myth has never been substantiated,

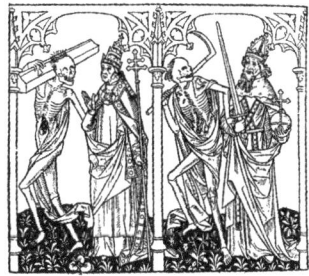

but remains part of the legend of Countess Báthory, along with several missing personal diaries detailing the murders. She was apprehended in 1610 and immured in a tower where she remained for four years, until her death on August 21, 1614.

THE HAUNTING OF HILL HOUSE

A TALE OF SUBTLE psychological terror, Shirley Jackson's *The Haunting of Hill House* (1959) is one of the finest ghost stories of the late 20th century. Dr. Montague is an investigator of supernatural events seeking to prove the existence of paranormal activity at Hill House. He invites several carefully chosen people to stay at the manor in the hopes of stirring up something spooky. One of the visitors, the reclusive and damaged Eleanor Vance, relates the story through her fragile psyche. She believes the house is alive and targeting her. Sure enough, many uncanny events constellate around Eleanor, but it also becomes increasingly clear that she cannot be trusted as a reliable narrator, which only makes the read more unnerving. Is the house truly evil and causing the changes in the characters that Eleanor thinks she is witnessing? Or is Eleanor herself, in fact, haunting Hill House? The great news is, we never find out. *The Haunting of Hill House* is evocative of classic Henry James (*The Turn of the Screw*). It presents a puzzle of identity that emphasizes terror over horror and is a theme that Stephen King would recycle in his famous malevolent sentient house tale, *The Shining*. *The Haunting of Hill House* has been adapted for screen twice: once masterfully by Robert Wise in 1963 as *The Haunting*, and again, rather terribly, in 1999.

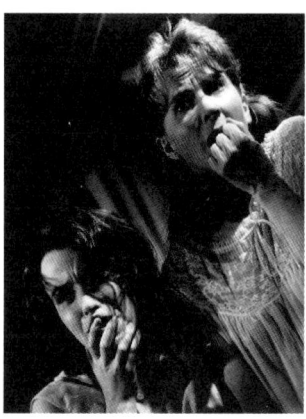

THE TURN OF THE SCREW

ONE OF THE FINEST GHOST STORIES ever written, Henry James' *The Turn of the Screw* (1898) is steeped in ambiguity and nuance. It begins conventionally enough: several friends share ghost stories around a fire one snowy Christmas Eve. One of them tells a suspenseful tale about a governess who believes her seaside country home is haunted by ghosts—that no else can see. She begins to wonder if everyone, including the children and servants are lying. Or is she losing her mind? This chilling tale has been adapted many times for screen, most recently with *The Others* (2001), but never quite so masterfully as 1961's *The Innocents*.

> "There is a lovely little horror story about the peasant who started through the haunted wood—the wood that was, people said, inhabited by devils who took any mortal who came their way. But the peasant thought, as he walked slowly along: 'I am a good man and have done no wrong. If devils can harm me, then there isn't any justice.' A voice behind him said, 'There isn't.'"
>
> FREDRIC BROWN (1906-1972), *US writer*

ON THE ORIGIN OF HORROR FICTION: THE CASTLE OF OTRANTO

THE ROOTS OF HORROR FICTION as we know it can be traced back to the 18TH century—the so-called "Age of Reason"—with Gothic fiction. Generally regarded as the first Gothic novel in the English language, Horace Walpole's *The Castle of Otranto* (1764) is an overtly Shakespearean tale that marries the 18TH century realist romance (which presented characters as real people in real situations) with the fantastic (unexplained or supernatural happenings). In this way it is aesthetically similar to magical realism, in which extraordinary things happen in ordinary situations, without explanation. To wit: Isabella is engaged to marry Conrad, heir to throne and Castle of Otranto. But when a giant helmet falls from the sky, killing Conrad, his father Manfred divorces his wife and attempts to claim Isabella for his own. She escapes the maze-like castle with a peasant named Theodore, who turns out to be the true Prince of Otranto. In his ruthless attempt to preserve his bloodline, Manfred ends up killing his own daughter.

In the book, real occurrences (wedding preparations) are presented in as straightforward a manner as fantastic occurrences (a giant helmet falling from the sky and landing on Conrad; a sighing portrait; supernaturally waving plumes of smoke). Here, Walpole introduces many set pieces and motifs that would later characterize the Gothic novel: the medieval setting, a vast, oppressive castle with a labyrinthine network of subterranean vaults and passages; an imperiled heroine fleeing a licentious male figure; strange sounds and doors opening by themselves; along with heavy doses of melodrama and parody. This range of narrative conventions would later exert a considerable influence over many writers at the apex of the Gothic movement including Charles Robert Maturin, Ann Radcliffe, Bram Stoker, Mary Shelley, Edgar Allan Poe, and Daphne du Maurier. The novel was loosely adapted into a film by renowned Czech director Jan Švankmajer in 1976. The filmmaker went on to adapt other classic horror works such as *The Pit and The Pendulum* and *Faust*.

THÉÂTRE DU GRAND GUIGNOL

FOUNDED BY OSCAR MÉTÉNIER, *Grand Guignol* (The Big Puppet Show) opened its doors in 1897 at 20 bis, rue Chaptal in Paris, France. A former chapel in the heart of the red light district, its purpose was to offer "naturalistic horror entertainment." In short, it was the original shock theatre; the height of Parisian sleaze, featuring low rent but high horror spectacles of violence and brutality in one-act plays between 10-40 minutes in length. With just 285 seats, theatre patrons were likely to end up splattered in blood and gore. In this way, *Grand Guignol* was one of the progenitors of practical make-up effects with its realistic beheadings, disembowlings and other illusory brutalities. *Guignol* was named after a traditional Lyonnaise puppet character and became one of the leading adult tourist attractions in the French capital for 65 years until its eventual demise in 1962. But its influence on horror cinema can be seen as early as the German Expressionist movement all the way to the Italian giallo, the American slasher, and the recent "torture porn" movement. The phrase "Grand Guignol" has even been adopted into the English language to describe any violent spectacle. The outrageous, gore-themed theatrics of the band GWAR can also be described contemporary "Grand Guignol-esque."

SELECTED POEMS OF EDGAR ALLAN POE

| AL AARAAF (1829) |
| THE BELLS (1849) |
| ANNABEL LEE (1849) |
| THE CITY IN THE SEA (1831) |
| THE CONQUEROR WORM (1843) |
| A DREAM WITHIN A DREAM (1849) |
| ELDORADO (1849) |
| EULALIE (1845) |
| THE HAUNTED PALACE (1839) |
| TO HELEN (1848) |
| LENORE (1843) |
| TAMERLANE (1829) |
| THE RAVEN (1845) |
| ULALUME (1847) |

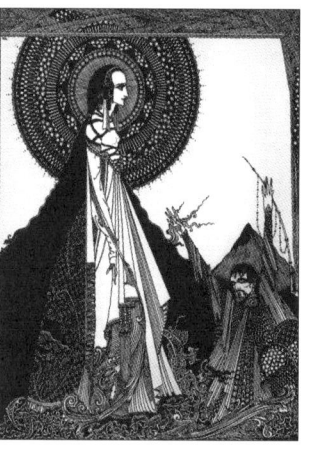

STEPHEN KING

Back in 1973, Tabitha King fished a three-page manuscript out of the trash bin in her husband's office. She read the piece, a shower scene about a telekinetic teenage girl who is pelted with sanitary napkins by her peers while on her period, and handed it back to him. At his wife's insistence, Stephen King finished the novel and submitted it to Doubleday, who published it on April 5, 1974. The book, entitled *Carrie*, sold four million copies. And that's the story of how a poor girl with menstrual problems made Stephen King a household name. He went on to write some of the most important modern horror novels and short stories, including: *Salem's Lot* (1975), *The Shining* (1977), *The Stand* (1978), *The Dead Zone* (1979), *Firestarter* (1980), *Cujo* (1981), *Christine* (1983), *Pet Sematary* (1983), *The Skeleton Crew* (1985), *It* (1986), *Misery* (1987), *Needful Things* (1991), *The Green Mile* (1996), *Bag of Bones* (1998), *Cell* (2006), and *Full Dark, No Stars* (2010). He also co-wrote the DC Comics/Vertigo comic book series, *American Vampire* (2011).

THE BOOKS OF BLOOD

"Everybody is a book of blood; wherever we're opened, we're red." The opening line of Clive Barker's 1984 collection of short stories sets the reader up for the six-book journey ahead. Wherever Barker takes you, you can be sure of one thing: there will be blood.

The British author made his horror debut with *The Books of Blood* (1984-1985) a collection of exquisitely perverse "splatterpunk" tales that caught the attention of Stephen King, who dubbed Barker "the future of horror." He couldn't have been more correct in his prophecy because Barker went on to achieve international acclaim in 1987 with *Hellraiser* (a film he directed from a novella called *The Hellbound Heart*) and become one of the most important horror fantasy figures in the genre.

The stories run the gamut of sex and violence, both supernatural and visceral. From the homoerotic, *In the Hills, The Cities*, to the body horror of *Jacqueline Ess: Her Will and Testament*, *The Books of Blood* collection is Barker at his most unrestrained. Several films have been adapted from *The Books of Blood* including *Rawhead Rex* (1986), *Candyman* (1992), *Lord of Illusions* (1995), *Quicksilver Highway* (1997), *The Midnight Meat Train* (2008), *The Book of Blood* (2008), and *Dread* (2009). Other classic Barker Books include, *The Damnation Game* (1985), *Weaveworld* (1987), *Cabal* (1988), *Imajica* (1991), and the first two parts of the "Art Trilogy" of *The Great and Secret Show* (1989) and *Everville* (1994).

ESSENTIAL LOVECRAFTIAN FILMS

THE LONESOME DEATH OF JORDY VERRILL segment in *Creepshow* (dir. George A. Romero, 1982)

ALIEN (dir. Ridley Scott, 1979)

BRIDE OF RE-ANIMATOR (dir. Brian Yuzna, 1989)

CITY OF THE LIVING DEAD (dir. Lucio Fulci, 1980)

DAGON (dir. Stuart Gordon, 2001)

DEAD & BURIED (dir. Gary Sherman, 1981)

EVIL DEAD II (dir. Sam Raimi, 1987)

FROM BEYOND (dir. Stuart Gordon, 1986)

HELLBOY (dir. Guillermo del Toro, 2004)

HELLBOY II: THE GOLDEN ARMY (dir. Guillermo del Toro, 2008)

HOUSE BY THE CEMETERY (dir. Lucio Fulci, 1981)

IN THE MOUTH OF MADNESS (dir. John Carpenter, 1994)

LEMORA: A CHILD'S TALE OF THE SUPERNATURAL (dir. Richard Blackburn, 1973)

MAREBITO (dir. Takashi Shimizu, 2004)

PRINCE OF DARKNESS (dir. John Carpenter, 1987)

PROMETHEUS (dir. Ridley Scott, 2012)

QUATERMASS AND THE PIT (dir. Roy Ward Baker, 1967)

RE-ANIMATOR (dir. Stuart Gordon, 1985)

THE BEYOND (dir. Lucio Fulci, 1981)

THE CRAWLING EYE (dir. Quentin Lawrence, 1958)

THE EVIL DEAD (dir. Sam Raimi, 1981)

THE FOG (dir. John Carpenter, 1980)

THE MIST (dir. Frank Darabont, 2007)

THE THING (dir. John Carpenter, 1982)

UZUMAKI (dir. Higuchinsky, 2000)

IN THE BEGINNING

HUMANS BY NATURE are storytelling mammals. Ever since we first huddled around a fire, we've been telling stories about the dark and what lives inside it. Tales that we might categorize today as "speculative fiction." Horror has an ancient history that is difficult to map but it appears throughout the historical record in creation myths and classical mythologies, which are festooned with monsters, demons, and otherworldly creatures. The bestselling book of all time, *The Bible*, could easily be labeled as horror, as it is populated by fallen angels, demonic possession, ghosts, zombies, and even a terrifying apocalypse! That's pretty good terror value for one novel.

THE NIGHTMARE

THIS 1781 GOTHIC OIL PAINTING by Swiss born artist Henry Fuseli (1741–1825) depicts a dreamer and her nightmares (an incubus and mare's head) in the same special environment. It is thought to have been an influence on Mary Shelley's *Frankenstein* (1818) and Edgar Allan Poe's short story, *The Fall of the House of Usher* (1839). The painting, or imagery taken from it, appears in both stories.

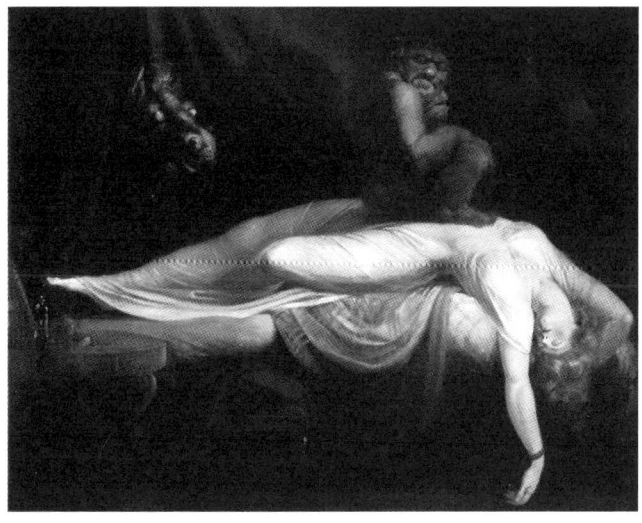

THE DIVINE COMEDY (1308-1321)

ALTHOUGH NOT typically included in the timeline of horror, Dante Alighieri's *The Divine Comedy* (Italian: *Divina Commedia*) includes one of the most expansive and influential descriptions of Hell in literature. It is a semi-autobiographical epic poem that describes Dante's travels through "Hell," "Purgatory" and "Paradise." Moreover, it is an allegory of a soul's ascent to God. By far the most popular edition features the eerie woodcuts of French engraver Paul Gustave Doré, with its haunting depictions of sinners' torment in Hell. Doré also contributed engravings to Edgar Allan Poe's *The Raven* (1884), Milton's *Paradise Lost* (1866), and Coleridge's *The Rime of the Ancient Mariner* (1873).

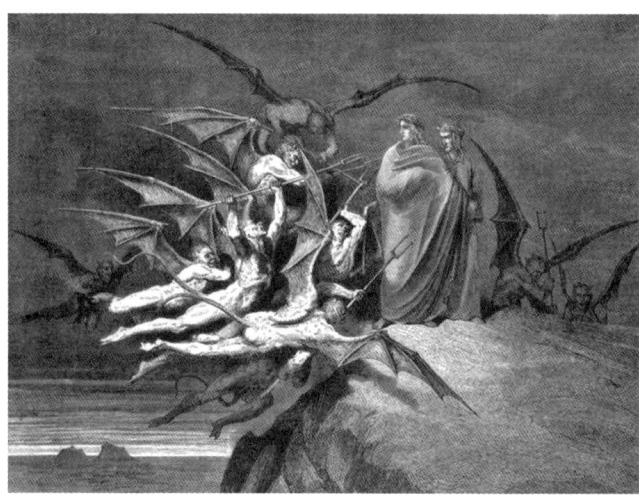

LORD OF THE FLIES

CIVILITY SLIPS AWAY from a group of shipwrecked schoolboys who regress into savagery in William Golding's Nobel prize-winning, *Lord of the Flies* (1954). The book was a huge influence on Stephen King, who borrowed the locale "Castle Rock" as the name of a fictional town that appears in several of his stories. *Lord of the Flies* has been adapted for film twice and served as the inspiration for many films including Kinji Fukasaku's blood-drenched, *Battle Royale* (2000) and the Hollywood blockbuster, *The Hunger Games* (2012).

A DECADENT READER

THE FLOWERS OF EVIL (LES FLEURS DU MAL)
—Charles Baudelaire (1857)

AGAINST NATURE (À REBOURS)—Joris-Karl Huysmans (1884)

LA HORLA—Guy de Maupassant (1886)

THE DECAY OF LYING—Oscar Wilde (1889)

THE PICTURE OF DORIAN GRAY—Oscar Wilde (1891)

MONSIEUR DE PHOCAS—Jean Lorrain (1901)

H.P. LOVECRAFT

HOWARD PHILLIPS LOVECRAFT WAS BORN on August 20, 1890 at 194 Angell Street in Providence, Rhode Island. His syphilitic father, Winfield Scott Lovecraft, was committed to a mental asylum when Howard was three years old. He was a sickly child, left in the custody of his overprotective mother, Sarah Susan Phillips, who lived with her father and two sisters. Lovecraft's grandfather Whipple Van Buren Phillips encouraged his budding literary talent (poetry) while his mother dressed him in girl's clothing and kept him away from school. He finally entered school aged eight, only to be withdrawn because of his ongoing illness. His emotional well-being was shattered when Whipple died in 1904. His family was forced to move due to mismanagement of Whipple's estate and Howard entered a five-year period of suicidal depression. In 1909, Lovecraft's mother was committed to the same hospital his father died in. Slowly, he found his way back to writing, to New York, and a brief marriage to fellow writer Sonia Haft Greene, seven years his senior. But Lovecraft hated New York life. His inability to find any paying work amidst the massive immigrant population brought out his racist leanings and general xenophobia—something that would become an all-encompassing motif in his writing. After his marriage failed, Lovecraft retreated to live with his aunts in Providence for the last decade of his life, where he would write his seminal tales of genre-defining "cosmic horror," primarily for *Weird Tales* magazine. He died on March 15, 1937 from a long, painful battle with intestinal cancer. He was 47 years old. The influence of Robert W. Chambers, Lord Dunsany, Arthur Machen, and Edgar Allan Poe loom large in Lovecraft's stories. His writing style is often in found manuscript form, pretentious and loaded with archaisms that alienated younger readers. And, like Poe, he didn't become a genre superstar until well after he was dust and bones.

H.P. LOVECRAFT: RECOMMENDED READING

THE TOMB (1917)
DAGON (1917)
THE STATEMENT OF RANDOLPH CARTER (1919)
THE TEMPLE (1920)
FROM BEYOND (1920)
THE MUSIC OF ERICH ZANN (1921)
THE OUTSIDER (1921)
THE LURKING FEAR (1922)
THE HOUND (1922)
THE RATS IN THE WALLS (1923)
THE SHUNNED HOUSE (1924)
THE CALL OF CTHULHU (1926)
THE SILVER KEY (1926)
PICKMAN'S MODEL (1926)
THE COLOR OUT OF SPACE (1927)
THE CASE OF CHARLES DEXTER WARD (1927)
THE DREAM-QUEST OF UNKNOWN KADATH (1927)
THE DUNWICH HORROR (1928)
THE WHISPERER IN DARKNESS (1930)
AT THE MOUNTAINS OF MADNESS (1931)
THE SHADOW OVER INNSMOUTH (1931)
THE DREAMS IN THE WITCH HOUSE (1932)
THE HAUNTER OF THE DARK (1935)
THE SHADOW OUT OF TIME (1935)

> "When I was nine I played the demon king in Cinderella and it launched me on a long and happy life of being a monster."
> BORIS KARLOFF (1887-1969), *UK actor*

HORROR VS. TERROR

IN THE GENRE, HORROR AND TERROR have two very different meanings. Gothic writer Ann Radcliffe (1764–1823) was the one of the first to address this distinction and draw a dividing line in the emergent genre of Gothic fiction—a genre she helped define with the archetypal gothic tale, *The Mysteries of Udopho* (1794). In an 1826 essay, *On the Supernatural in Poetry*, she regards horror as the fear of something that one is aware is happening or going to happen, whereas terror is a fear of the unknown. In fact, she insists they are polar opposites: "Terror and Horror are so far opposite that the first expands the soul, and awakens the faculties to a high degree of life; the other contracts, freezes, and nearly annihilates them … And where lies the difference between horror and terror, but in the uncertainty and obscurity that accompany the first, respecting the dreaded evil?" Radcliffe was in part responding and objecting to the lurid excesses in Matthew Gregory Lewis' transgressive Gothic novel *The Monk* (1796), which, incidentally, is the first book to feature a priest as a villain (an inspiration for *The Hunchback of Notre Dame*). While *The Monk* shares some of the traits of *The Mysterious of Udolpho*, Radcliffe felt it relished too much in the excesses of horror (gore, violence), whereas her tales were rooted firmly in terror (the unknown).

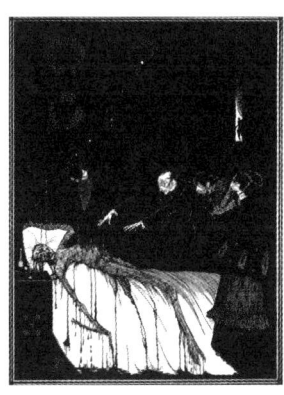

One of the first critics to adopt her use of terror and horror to illustrate the difference between these two types of Gothic fiction was Devendra P. Varma, who said in *The Gothic Flame* (1966), "The difference between Terror and Horror is the difference between awful apprehension and sickening realization: between the smell of death and stumbling against a corpse."

NIGHTMARE USA

EVERYTHING YOU EVER WANTED to know about American exploitation films and more is in Stephen Thrower's indispensable coffee-table-crushing book, *Nightmare USA*. Drenched in blood and other bodily fluids, this chronological history of underground exploitation and horror cinema is by the world's foremost authority. From *Abducted* (1973), to *Zombie Island Massacre* (1983), it's all here. A must own for any true horror cinephile.

TOP 5 GEORGE ROMERO FILMS

1 MARTIN (1976): Martin doesn't have fangs but he has a razor blade and syringes that do the trick. One of the best vampire films ever made.

2 DAY OF THE DEAD (1985): A criminally underrated claustrophobic sequel featuring spectacular gore FX.

3 CREEPSHOW (1982): Romero directs and Stephen King writes this famous EC Comics-styled horror anthology. Frightening and funny.

4 NIGHT OF THE LIVING DEAD (1968): Inverts nearly every convention of the traditional horror film. A landmark zombie film.

5 DAWN OF THE DEAD (1979): The survivors get along much better than *Night*'s group, but they still can't escape other humans, who turn out to be the real threat to their safety.

MEN, WOMEN, AND CHAINSAWS

CAROL CLOVER'S FAMOUS 1992 ACADEMIC examination of gender in modern horror cinema takes a distinctly feminist approach, but not the one you might expect. Instead of lambasting mean-spirited films such as *I Spit on Your Grave* (1978) as indefensible exercises misogyny, Clover stands up for the slasher, exploitation, and "rape and revenge" subgenres, arguing that these oft-dismissed films possess value as subversive gender studies, in which the audience identifies with the (usually female) victim and not the (usually male) killer. Although they are sadistic, Clover points out these films often feature women empowering themselves against their male oppressors, most notably in her observation of what she calls the "Final Girl," a common slasher film trope. The Final Girl is usually a smart, resourceful woman who ends up besting the killer and is the only remaining survivor of the ordeal. Examples of Final Girls include *Halloween*'s Laurie Strode, *Alien*'s Lt. Ripley, *A Nightmare on Elm Street*'s Nancy Thompson, and *Friday the 13TH*'s Alice Hardy.

PSYCHO

ED GEIN WAS ARRESTED ON NOVEMBER 16, 1957 for the murders of two women. Upon entering his home in Plainfield, Wisconsin, police discovered he had furnished his home with human remains. In addition to the heads of two women he had murdered and cannibalized, authorities found furniture, clothing, masks, and even cutlery, made from human body parts and skin. Gein admitted to grave robbing for females roughly the same age and appearance of his dead mother, a controlling puritan who thought all women, herself excluded, were whores and instruments of the devil. He also told police psychiatrists that he decided he wanted a sex change. They presumed Gein was using the remains he pillaged from graves to fashion a female skin suit, in a reach to become his own dead mother.

Author Robert Bloch was living 35 miles away in nearby Weyauwega when the news broke about Gein's crimes. Inspired by "the notion that the man next door may be a monster unsuspected even in the gossip-ridden microcosm of small-town life," Bloch began writing a book based on the circumstances of the Gein case. The result was *Psycho*, a thriller about a cross-dressing grave robber who is so obsessed with his mother that he develops a murderous personality for her in his own mind. The actual details of the Gein case were too grisly to be released to the public and Bloch was shocked when he "discovered how closely the imaginary character I'd created resembled the real Ed Gein both in overt act and apparent motivation."

Published in 1959, *Psycho* was a critical success, earning the author the prestigious Hugo Award the same year. The story relied on the horror of interior psychology as opposed to the supernatural, which appealed to readers at the time. Said Bloch, "I realized, as a result of what went on during World War II and of reading the more widely disseminated work in psychology, that the real horror is not in the shadows, but in that twisted little world inside our own skulls." The rights to the story were sold to an anonymous bidder for $9,500 (of which the author received $6,750). The film, called *Psycho*, was released the following year from director Alfred Hitchcock. It featured unprecedented scenes of sexuality and violence, particularly in the infamous shower scene. It was nominated for four Academy Awards and is Hitchcock's best-known film and early precursor of the slasher subgenre, alongside Michael Powell's *Peeping Tom* (1960).

"My dear old monster. I owe everything to him. He's my best friend."
BORIS KARLOFF (1887-1969), *UK actor*

BRAM STOKER BIBLIOGRAPHY

THE PRIMROSE PATH (1875)

THE SNAKE'S PASS (1890)

THE WATTER'S MOU' (1895)

THE SHOULDER OF SHASTA (1895)

DRACULA (1897)

MISS BETTY (1898)

THE MYSTERY OF THE SEA (1902)

THE JEWEL OF THE SEVEN STARS (1903)

THE MAN (1905)

LADY ATHLYNE (1908)

THE LADY OF THE SHROUD (1909)

THE LAIR OF THE WHITE WORM (1911)

DRACULA'S GUEST (1914)

THE HUNCHBACK OF NOTRE-DAME

VICTOR HUGO'S TRAGIC 1831 LOVE STORY is the original beauty and the beast tale. After offering him a drink of water, deformed church bell-ringer Quasimodo falls deeply in love with a popular gypsy named Esmerelda. She quickly falls out of favor with the public and is eventually accused of being a witch. In a dramatic rescue, Quasimodo swoops in to save her. It is not long before she is betrayed yet again and eventually murdered. If what Quasimodo does next doesn't melt your heart, you don't have one. Famously adapted for cinema in 1923, starring Lon Chaney as Quasimodo and again in 1939 with Charles Laughton as The Hunchback. The two films are considered to be the best adaptations of Hugo's novel.

> *"Horror is like a serpent; always shedding its skin, always changing. And it will always come back. It can't be hidden away like the guilty secrets we try to keep in our subconscious."*
>
> DARIO ARGENTO (BORN 1940),
> *Italian director, producer, and writer*

FAMOUS MONSTERS OF FILMLAND

FAMOUS MONSTERS hit the stands in 1958, edited by fantastic film enthusiast and rabid collector, Forrest J Ackerman. The magazine capitalized on the success of classic horror films that were being broadcast on television at the time. No one could have predicted just how popular those black and white films would be among children.

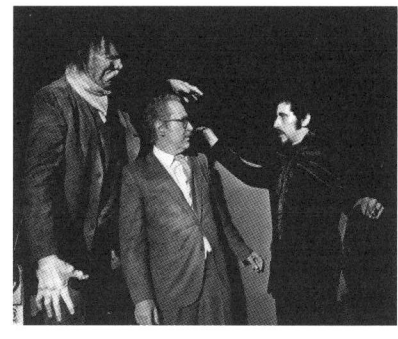

In the magazine, Ackerman (AKA "Forry," or "The Ackermonster") spoke directly to these creature-loving "Monster Kids" through silly puns, and to adults through full-page photos of movie monsters, imploring parents to permit children to indulge their imaginations because in "Horrorwood, Karloffornia," monsters were actually good for you. It was a safe, fun, and exciting publication. You'd never know its editor was a nudist!

Famous Monsters also single handedly sparked fan and collector culture with its popular mail order ads. These lurid classifieds teemed with monster masks, make-up and model kits, skeleton hands, talking skulls, and even the opportunity to own your very own monster fly—delights few Monster Kids could resist, especially Forry, the biggest collector of them all. The walls of his infamous home, "The Ackermansion," were festooned with collectables and monster movie memorabilia—all open to the public. He helped organize the very first science fiction conventions, dressed in costume (which became cosplay), discovered Ray Bradbury, and even coined the term "sci-fi." After 191 issues the magazine closed in 1983. It was resurrected in 1993, but sadly ended up in a civil libel lawsuit that Forry won against the new editor. The magazine was never the same after Forry's departure.

Still, the influence of the first run of Famous Monsters on that generation of monster kids immeasurable, many of whom grew up to be pioneers in their own right. Directors Joe Dante (*Gremlins*), John Landis (*An American Werewolf in London*), Peter Jackson (*The Lord of the Rings*), Steven Spielberg (*Jaws*), George Lucas (*Star Wars*), and Frank Darabont (*The Mist*) all count themselves as Uncle Forry's monster kids. Without Famous Monsters there would be no later horror magazines such as *Fangoria*. Forry died on December 4, 2008 at the age of 92. And although the publication persists in a new format, *Famous Monsters of Filmland* died with Forry that day.

EDGAR ALLAN POE

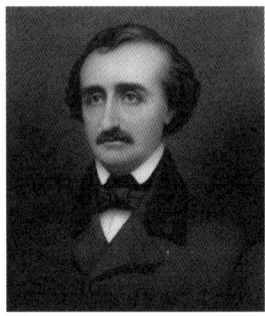

EDGAR POE WAS BORN TO itinerant actors David and Elizabeth Poe in Boston on January 19, 1809. To say he lived a troubled life is an understatement. The trouble started early. In 1810, Edgar's father abandoned Elizabeth and their three children, who were orphaned after their mother died of consumption (pulmonary tuberculosis) when Edgar was just two years old. The siblings were separated and sent to three different homes. Edgar became the ward of a rich merchant named John Allan from Richmond, Virginia. Allan never legally adopted Edgar, nor did he love him like a son (his wife Fanny was unable to bear children of their own) but he did foster him, give him a new name, and put him through school for a while. Shortly after enrolling in the University of Virginia, Poe began drinking, gambling, and getting into trouble. After accruing a large gambling debt, he was expelled for not paying his gambling debts and forced to move back to Boston, severing his financial ties with John Allan. By this time Poe had already anonymously published a book of poems, *Tamerlane and Other Poems* (1827), and set out to make a living as a full-time writer. He took several jobs as magazine editor, newspaper writer, and clerk but was unable to keep any of them for very long due to his love affair with drink and his obdurate personality. Unable to make ends meet, he enrolled in the army in 1827 under an assumed name, but soon had himself dismissed. By October of 1830, he was disowned by John Allan and fired from his job as an assistant editor at the *Southern Literary Messenger*, for constant drunkenness. He eventually alienated himself from everyone, including the literary establishment by publicly accusing Henry Wadsworth Longfellow of plagiarism. In September of 1835, Poe secretly married his 13 year-old cousin Virginia Clemm—muse for his masterful poem, *The Raven* (1845)—who died 13 years later of tuberculosis aggravated by abject poverty that Poe was unable to alleviate with his writing, despite many reprints of his work. On October 3, 1849, Poe was found drunk, delirious, and wandering the streets of Baltimore in someone else's clothes. He died in hospital on October 7, 1849. To this day no one knows how he ended up in such a state, nor the true cause of death. Rumours include syphilis, meningitis, rabies, alcoholism, suicide, cholera, and heart disease. Poe has for many years been considered the father of the detective story and a landmark figure in short horror fiction. He revolutionized the Gothic horror story, endowing it with painfully artful atmosphere and psychological dismay.

THE CALL OF CTHULHU

FIRST PUBLISHED IN THE February 1928 issue of *Weird Tales* magazine, *The Call of Cthulhu* is H.P. Lovecraft's best-known short story and most intense expression of mankind's insignificance in the universe, as indicated in the first sentence: "The most merciful thing in the world, I think, is the inability of the human mind to correlate all its contents. We live on a placid island of ignorance in the midst of black seas of infinity; and it was not meant that we should voyage far." It is also the only story in which the now infamous eponymous extraterrestrial deity makes a major appearance.

Lovecraft's unique brand of sanity-destroying cosmic horror is often told in documentary format, through a secondary source. In this case, the nephew of a deceased professor reads a manuscript, "found among the papers of the late Francis Wayland Thurston, of Boston." The text reveals the existence of a cult capable of awakening an ancient slumbering evil from its watery depths. Once awakened, this monster, known as "Cthulhu," will usher in an era "free and wild and beyond good and evil, with laws and morals thrown aside and all men shouting and killing and reveling in joy"—to the detriment of all living things, presumably. Much to the narrator's horror, he realizes the cult actually exists, that the deed has already been done and that he already knows too much.

The Call of Cthulhu is the best introduction to the Cthulhu mythos and Lovecraftian lore in general. While his work was not very popular in his lifetime, Lovecraft is acknowledged as one of the greatest practitioners of horror fiction. His influence on the genre and popular culture is as immeasurable and pervasive as Cthulhu's malevolence. One can only imagine the mind-melting terror Lovecraft would experience knowing his cosmic entity has been made into plush toys, cake toppers, and even cute fuzzy slippers.

MORE KONG

KING KONG (dir. Merian C. Cooper, 1933)

THE SON OF KONG (dir. Ernest B. Schoedsack, 1933)

KING KONG VS. GODZILLA (dir. Ishirō Honda, 1962)

KING KONG ESCAPES (dir. Ishirō Honda, 1967)

KING KONG (dir. John Guillermin, 1976)

KING KONG LIVES (dir. John Guillermin, 1986)

KING KONG (dir. Peter Jackson, 2005)

HEART OF DARKNESS

"He cried in a whisper at some image, at some vision—he cried out twice, a cry that was no more than a breath—'The horror! The horror!'" Joseph Conrad's 1902 exploration of the darkness potentially inherent in all human hearts is a gripping masterpiece that exposes the horrors of colonialism in the African Congo. A pessimistic but compulsory read.

LUCIO FULCI

WHEN IT COMES TO ITALIAN horror, two names immediately come to mind: Dario Argento and Lucio Fulci. Of course there are dozens of lesser-known spaghetti horror practitioners worth discussing, but these two have achieved the most notoriety on the global cinema stage. And oddly, people tend to favor one over the other.

Ironically, Fucli got his start directing comedies, about 18 of them in fact, before making his first gialli with *Lizard in a Woman's Skin* (1969) and *Don't Torture a Duckling* (1972). Before long, he developed a trademark that set him apart from Argento: extreme gore effects. Fulci's films were loaded with intensely graphic special effects sequences so realistic he ended up in court facing animal cruelty charges (for *Lizard...*).

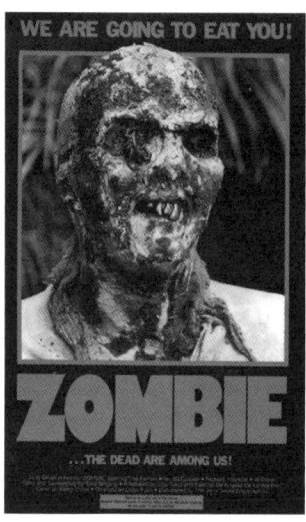

Fucli is most well known for his zombie films. *Zombie* (1979) was released in Italy as *Zombi 2* in an attempt to capitalize on the success of Romero's *Dawn of the Dead* (released in Italy as *Zombie*). The marketing ploy worked because *Zombi 2* got Fulci international recognition. Later, he made a trio of unforgettable supernatural horror films characterized by oneiric logic and, yes, plenty of extreme violence. *City of the Living Dead* (1980), *The Beyond* (1981), and *The House by the Cemetery* (1981), form a triptych of films loosely connected by a "Gates of Hell" theme. They are among his finest achievements, bolstered by composer Fabio Frizzi's creepy electronic soundscapes.

10 GREAT HORROR SEQUELS

1 THE EXORCIST III: LEGION (dir. William Peter Blatty, 1990): Features one of the scariest scenes in the history of horror cinema. The devil is truly in the details here, and this movie warrants repeat viewing.

2 AMITYVILLE II: THE POSSESSION (dir. Damiano Damiani, 1982): This over-the-top "prequel" has an icky and totally perverse flavor, courtesy of Italian director Damiani.

3 BRIDE OF FRANKENSTEIN (dir. James Whale, 1935): A rare example of a sequel that is superior to its predecessor.

4 DAY OF THE DEAD (dir. George Romero, 1985): One of the most overlooked films in the "Of the Dead" series. Slow, but incredibly gory.

5 FRIDAY THE 13TH: THE FINAL CHAPTER (dir. Joseph Zito, 1984): The fan favorite in which a pre-pubescent Cory Feldman gives it to Jason like nobody's business.

6 THE TEXAS CHAINSAW MASSACRE 2 (dir. Tobe Hooper, 1986): This high camp horror comedy sequel is ridiculously lovable.

7 PHANTASM II (dir. Don Coscarelli, 1988): Fast cars, ghouls, and guns. What more could you ask for in a horror sequel?

8 HELLBOUND: HELLRAISER II (dir. Tony Randel, 1988): Clive Barker's notorious "Sadomasochists from Beyond the Grave" return to recapture a horny, skinless Julia, who is using a doctor to become flesh again.

9 PSYCHO II (dir. Richard Franklin, 1983): Norman Bates is released from the nuthouse only to kill again . . . this time in color!

10 HALLOWEEN III: SEASON OF THE WITCH (dir. Tommy Lee Wallace, 1982): There is no masked killer in sight but there are head-melting Halloween masks, creepy cyborgs, and a couple of chilling Tom Atkins love scenes!

THE BLACK PAINTINGS

THOUGH HIS WORK ALWAYS LEANED toward the macabre, former Spanish court painter Francisco Goya created a series of 14 frescoes between 1819 and 1923 that depict unrivaled haunting imagery. Aged 74, near deaf, disillusioned, and quite misanthropic, Goya painted the disturbing black smears directly onto the plaster walls of his villa just outside of Madrid. These artworks, later transferred to canvas, are now known as *Las Pinturas Negras*, "*The Black Paintings*" and most notably include *Saturn Devouring His Son*, *Witches' Sabbath* and *Atropos (The Fates)*.

LIGHTS OUT

OLD-TIME RADIO'S MOST FAMOUS program of the weird and supernatural, *Lights Out* debuted at midnight on a Wednesday in January, 1934 on NBC's WENR. Series head Wyllis Cooper conceived the idea of "a midnight mystery serial to catch the attention of the listeners at the witching hour." And catch the attention of the listeners, he did. The show was originally a 15-minute program that was expanded to 30 minutes due to its overwhelming popularity. Gruesome sound effects were added to voice readings, which amped up the sensationalism and horror. Cooper left *Lights Out* in 1936 to write feature film scripts including *Son of Frankenstein* (1939). He was replaced by Arch Oboler, who hit the ground running with *Burial Services*, a story in which a paralyzed girl is buried alive. The segment caused a sensation and NBC received thousands of outraged letters from concerned listeners. As a result, Oboler became a household name, synonymous with horror. The show stopped and started several times (1934-1939, 1942-1943, 1945-1947) and featured the acting talents of Boris Karloff, Mercedes McCambridge, Raymond Edward Johnson, and Mason Adams.

> *"I think of horror films as art, as films of confrontation. Films that make you confront aspects of your own life that are difficult to face. Just because you're making a horror film doesn't mean you can't make an artful film."*
>
> DAVID CRONENBERG (BORN 1943),
> *Canadian director, producer, actor, and writer*

THE WORLD'S FIRST HORROR MOVIE

HERE IT IS, THE WORLD'S FIRST horror movie. Drum roll please . . . *La Manoir du Diable* (*The House of the Devil*) is a three-minute French film made in 1896 by special effects pioneer Georges Méliès, who also made the groundbreaking, *A Trip to The Moon*. Although it's about as scary as Disney's *Fantasia*, the film terrified audiences upon its release in Paris on Christmas Eve with its inventive visual trickery. The plot, as it were: A large bat flies into a medieval castle and transforms into a pantomiming Mephistopheles (played by Méliès). There he prepares a cauldron and produces from it several ghastly delights including witches, skeletons, and ghosts. The demon is, however, quickly spirited away by a heroic knight with a crucifix. *La Manoir du Diable* also ostensibly marks the first onscreen appearance of Satan, who would go on to have a long career in film.

NIGHT OF THE LIVING DEAD

WHILE THERE WERE PLENTY OF ZOMBIE movies that came before it, George Romero's *Night of the Living Dead* (1968) defined the subgenre more than any other. Borrowing from Richard Matheson's *I Am Legend*, Romero replaced the vampires in Matheson's seminal apocalyptic siege story with "ghouls" and set it in a farmhouse in rural Pennsylvania. A group of survivors hole up in the house and argue over what they should do as dead people continue to return to life all around them. It all goes badly as the group falls apart and its members become victims to the relentless flesh-hungry horde.

Until this point in cinema, most zombies had been depicted as the product of voodoo, mind control, or alien intelligence. Vegans, if you will. It is here that the zombie becomes a fully-fledged cannibal. More than that, it is a subversive masterpiece and a damning critique of American authority and its involvement in the Vietnam war. At the end of the film, social order is not restored, heroes are not rewarded for courage and the zombies are not vanquished, sending a clear message to viewers at the time: Everything is not okay.

Night of the Living Dead spawned a series of sequels of from Romero including *Dawn of the Dead* (1978), *Day of the Dead* (1985), *Land of the Dead* (2005), *Diary of the Dead* (2007), and *Survival of the Dead* (2009). He is regarded as the godfather of modern zombie cinema.

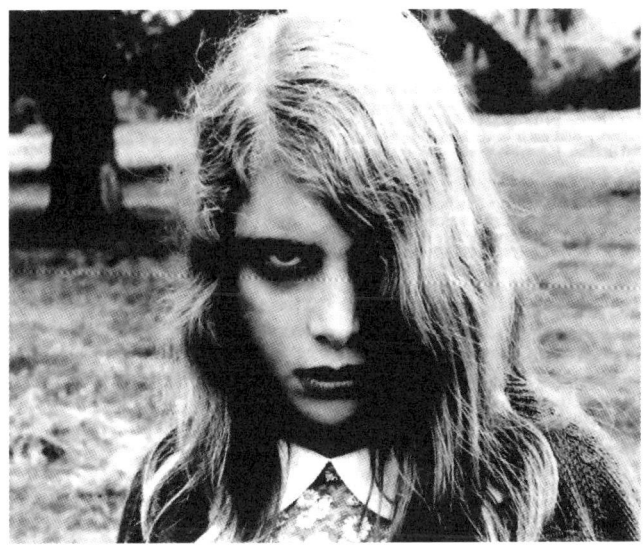

———— 5 MANDATORY RIPPER FILMS ————

1 THE LODGER (1926): Alfred Hitchcock's silent, atmospheric, and expressionist adaptation of Marie Belloc Lowndes' famous novel, *The Lodger* is the first Ripper film.

2 THE BOX OF PANDORA (1929): In this silent German melodrama, Louise Brooks stars as a naïve seductress whose carefree eroticism eventually brings ruin to her life and leads her into the arms of Jack the Ripper. Directed by Georg Wilhelm Pabst.

3 HANDS OF THE RIPPER (1971): Directed by Peter Sasdy (*Taste the Blood of Dracula*, *Countess Dracula*), this British Hammer film focuses on Jack the Ripper's fictional offspring, who gives new meaning to the phrase, "like father, like daughter."

4 MURDER BY DECREE (1979): Based on the book *Jack the Ripper: The Final Solution* by Stephen Knight, Bob Clark's British-Canadian film intermingles real and fictional characters from Arthur Conan Doyle's imagination. It stars Christopher Plummer and James Mason as Sherlock Holmes and Dr. John H. Watson, respectively, and was the first film to suggest royal and masonic involvement in the Ripper mystery.

5 FROM HELL (2002): Loosely based on Alan Moore and Eddie Campbell's 10-part comic book series of the same name, *From Hell* stars Johnny Depp as an opium-addicted police inspector who believes the Ripper murders are rooted in a masonic conspiracy. A miscast Heather Graham stars as Mary Kelly, a 17TH century prostitute with remarkably perfect teeth.

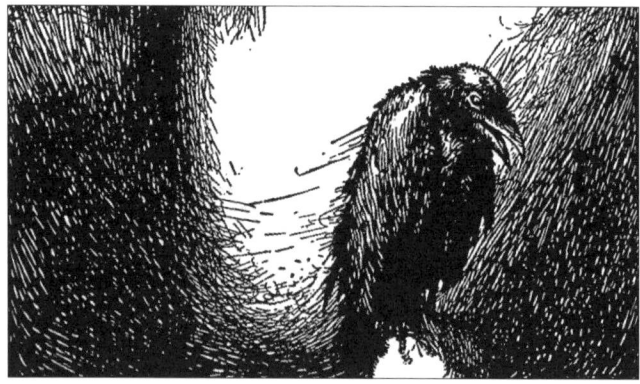

DRACULA

BRAM STOKER didn't invent the vampire, but he gave us Count Dracula, the most widely recognized fictional vampire in history. The plot, in short, delivered in epistolary format: English solicitor Jonathan Harker travels to Count Dracula's crumbling castle in the Carpathian mountains of Transylvania to facilitate a real estate sale for a house near London that the Count is interested in purchasing. Dracula takes a literal dirt nap and journeys to England on a Russian ship called the Demeter, which arrives completely devoid of life. The ship's logs reveal the presence of something sinister onboard. Dracula arrives and begins transferring the vampire plague to England. Beautiful Lucy Westenra is turned into a vampire and, quite memorably, is staked, beheaded, and stuffed with garlic—with the help of vampire hunter Abraham Van Helsing. Dracula himself is similarly dispatched following a suspenseful and tense race against the clock to save Harker's wife, Mina Murray. The 1897 book, of course, found favor with the press and has since been reprinted hundreds of times in many languages.

BORIS KARLOFF'S THRILLER

1949 WAS A MAGICAL YEAR for horror on television. The popular radio drama *Lights Out* had made the transition to TV in July that year, along with *Appointment with Fear* and *Suspense. Starring Boris Karloff* was a half hour anthology series that debuted on September 22, 1949 on the American Broadcast Company (ABC). The show aired on radio on Wednesdays, followed by a presentation of same story on television on Thursdays. This short-lived series was renamed *Mystery Playhouse Starring Boris Karloff* late in October of the same year. Sadly, not one of the 13 episodes survive. Karloff hosted another stillborn anthology series entitled *The Veil*, which never aired, before finally hitting pay dirt in 1960 with *Thriller*.

Thriller premiered on September 13, 1960 with the episode, *The Twisted Image*, and ran for two seasons that produced 67 episodes. The hour-long show was the best of its kind up to that point. With music from Jerry Goldsmith, Pete Rugolo, and Morton Stevens and horror heavyweight writers such as Robert E. Howard, Cornell Woolrich, Richard Matheson, and Robert Bloch—the show featured some of the most memorably terrifying hours of broadcast television. *Thriller* was shelved when Alfred Hitchcock brought an expanded one-hour version of *Alfred Hitchcock Presents* to NBC, but it remains beloved by genre fans and icons alike. In his non-fiction treatise on the horror genre, *Danse Macabre*, Stephen King calls *Thriller*, "the best horror series ever put on TV."

JUNJI ITO

JUNJI ITO (JULY 31, 1963) is a Japanese artist most well known for his bizarre, Lovecraftian body horror manga including the *Tomie* series, *Uzumaki, Gyo,* and *The Enigma of Amigara Fault*. Ito's tales (many of which have been adapted into exquisite films) are quite possibly the strangest and most grotesque to ever come out of Japan. Slug people, supernatural hair, and sharks with legs: this stuff will truly warp your mind.

DR. JEKYLL AND MR. HYDE

THE FIRST SCREEN adaptation of Robert Louis Stevenson's novel came with William N. Selig's now lost 1908 16-minute silent horror film, *Dr. Jekyll and Mr. Hyde*. It starred Hobart Bosworth as Jekyll/Hyde and featured a dramatic transformation sequence that shocked and impresses audiences. Not to be confused with *A Modern Dr. Jekyll,* a comedy released the same year, also written by Selig.

THE GODFATHER OF GORE

HERSCHELL GORDON LEWIS isn't just a filmmaker, he's also a businessman. His early career consisted of cheapjack sexploitation films, made more for profit than artistic expression. Lewis and his producing partner David F. Friedman shot dozens of nudie cuties and soft core exploitation dramas in the early 1960s before deciding to exploit a totally new avenue in low budget filmmaking: extreme blood and gore. The result was *Blood Feast* (1963), the first "splatter film," about a psychotic food caterer who kills people to prepare them in his recipes.

Cheap, tacky, and loaded with unprecedented full-color gore, *Blood Feast* (shot for $25,000) caused a sensation upon its release and was swiftly banned in some US states, which only stirred up more interest in the film on the grindhouse circuit. Lewis and Friedman realized they were on to something and took the profits from that film to shoot another gore film, *Two Thousand Maniacs!* (1964), about a Brigadoon-inspired magical town of Southern crazies who lure, torture, and kill Northern tourists. His final film with Friedman was 1965's *Color Me Blood Red*, about a murderous artist who uses his victims' blood as paint. Lewis made *A Taste of Blood* and *The Gruesome Twosome* on his own, two years later, and by the time *The Wizard of Gore* (1970) and *The Gore Gore Girls* (1972) were released, Lewis had overdone his career in gore films and retired from filmmaking altogether. 30 years later he returned to the subgenre he defined, with *Blood Feast II: All U Can Eat* (2002), an over-the-top splatter comedy that proved Lewis was still fit to be called "The Godfather of Gore."

THE STRANGE CASE OF DOCTOR JEKYLL AND MISTER HYDE

You know the story: A mad scientist concocts a potion and tries it on himself, only to turn into a violent monster. First published in 1886, *The Strange Case of Doctor Jekyll and Mister Hyde* is a Gothic mystery by Robert Louis Stevenson that tells the now famous story of a London lawyer, Mr. Utterson, who investigates the strange relationship between his friend Dr. Henry Jekyll and a mysterious and violent character known as Mr. Hyde. As it turns out Henry is suffering from dissociative identity disorder, an extremely rare mention condition commonly known as "split personality." There are now dozens of stage adaptations of the story with well over 100 film versions—most of them terrible— save for John S. Robertson's *Dr. Jekyll and Mr. Hyde* (1920), with a twisted-faced John Barrymore as Hyde (hands down, the screen's most terrifying version of the monster), and Robert Mamoulian's *Dr. Jekyll and Mr. Hyde* (1931) starring Frederic March as the titular character.

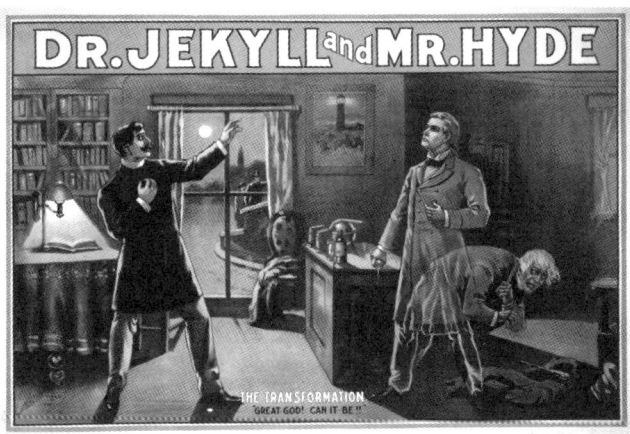

THE SHORTEST HORROR STORY

"THE LAST MAN ON EARTH sat alone in a room. There was a knock on the door…" This two-sentence story is only the beginning of Fredric Brown's *Knock*, originally published in the December 1948 issue of *Thrilling Wonder Stories*. It goes on to elaborate on who the last man is, but as a fragment, it's entirely complete, and perhaps even works better.

WEIRD TALES

THE FIRST ALL-FANTASY PULP MAGAZINE in the world launched in March 1923, with editor Edwin Baird at the helm. The magazine attracted a plethora of authors including Howard Phillips Lovecraft, Clark Ashton Smith, Robert Bloch, Robert E. Howard, Ray Bradbury, Manly Wade Wellman, Fritz Leiber, Theodore Sturgeon, and Joseph Payne Brennan. A public attempt to ban the November 1924 issue, because of a brief reference to necrophilia in C. M. Eddy's short story, *The Loved Dead*, only increased sales. The magazine survived 32 years despite ongoing financial problems. It was revived on numerous occasions, in 1974, 1984, 1988, and again in 2007. Other horror pulps—featuring lurid cover art—of the so-called "weird menace" era (also known as the "shudder pulps") included, *Terror Tales*, *Horror Stories*, *Strange Tales*, *Uncanny Tales*, *Eerie Stories,* and *Spicy Mystery Stories*.

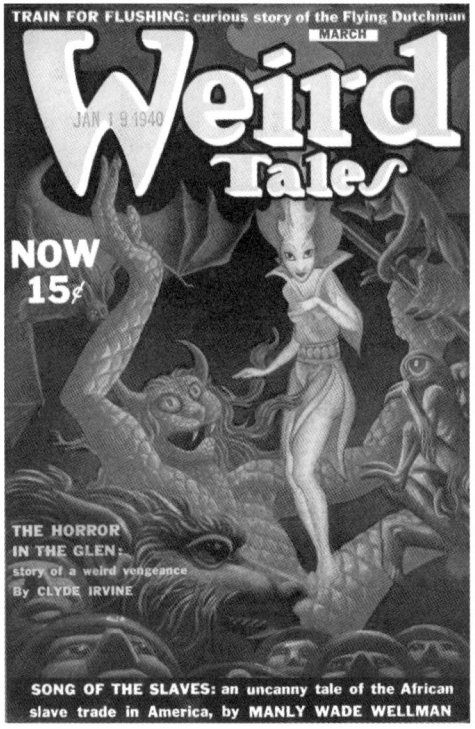

10 BEST HORROR MOVIE TAGLINES

1	"In space, no one can hear you scream." *Alien* (1979)
2	"Be afraid. Be very afraid." *The Fly* (1986)
3	"Herbert West has a very good head on his shoulders . . . And another one in a dish on his desk." *Re-Animator* (1985)
4	"If this one doesn't scare you, you're already dead!" *Phantasm* (1979)
5	"Trapped in time. Surrounded by evil. Low on gas." *Army of Darkness* (1992)
6	"When there's no more room in Hell, the dead will walk the Earth." *Dawn of the Dead* (1978)
7	"The lucky ones died first." *The Hills Have Eyes* (1977)
8	"Man is the warmest place to hide." *The Thing* (1982)
9	"Who will survive and what will be left of them?" *The Texas Chain Saw Massacre* (1974)
10	"The good news is your date is here! The bad news is . . . he's dead!" *Night of the Creeps* (1986)

TALES OF MOONLIGHT AND RAIN

JUST AS THE ENGLISH GOTHIC movement was getting its start, Japan had already published its first anthology of supernatural tales. In the 1776 book, *Tales of Moonlight and Rain* (*Ugetsu Monogatari*) Ueda Akinari spins nine spine-chilling yarns adapted from Chinese ghost stories of the Ming dynasty, recast as historical tales set in Japan. Highlights include *Aozukin* (*The Blue Hood*), about a homosexual priest who turns into a goblin; *Kibitsu no Kama* (*The Cauldron of Kibitsu*), about a scorned wife who possesses the body of the prostitute her husband ran off with; and *Asaji ga yado* (*House Amid the Thickets*), which formed the basis of the 1953 Kenji Mizoguchi film, *Ugetsu*.

> "People say that going to a horror movie is like a rollercoaster ride. But the rollercoaster ride analogy is limited. On a ride, you're only scared of being physically damaged. Horror films are a rollercoaster of the soul."
>
> GUILLERMO DEL TORO (BORN 1964)
> *Mexican writer, producer, and director*

JACK PIERCE

JACK PIERCE (BORN JANUS PICCOULA, 1889-1968) was Universal Pictures' full-time makeup man. After the death of Lon Chaney in 1930, a spot opened up for the Greek immigrant and erstwhile amateur baseball player, actor, and stuntman. Having impressed Universal head Carl Laemmle with his ape makeup on 1926's *The Monkey Talks*, Pierce was hired to give Conrad Veidt his sinister rictus-grin in *The Man Who Laughs* (1929). His most famous contribution to the studio's output was his work on Boris Karloff for *Frankenstein* (1931). The two collaborated on the arduous daily four-hour make-up application and design, with Karloff removing his dentures to create a concave indentation on one side of his face. Pierce built up Karloff's face with a grueling, toxic concoction of cotton, collodion (a nasty liquid plastic), gum adhesive and grease paint. The result was one of the most iconic movie make-ups in the history of cinema. They collaborated again on *The Mummy* the following year, and again in 1935 on *The Bride of Frankenstein*, where he revisited The Monster make-up and created a new icon with The Bride. Pierce was a stubborn man who was not comfortable using emerging makeup techniques. He did not begin using latex appliances until 1941 on *The Wolf Man*, starring Lon Chaney Jr. The two makeup men argued famously, with Chaney accusing Pierce of purposeful torture in the chair. Due to his difficult personality and refusal to adapt, Pierce was let go in 1949 by Universal, who wanted to start using faster, cheaper make-up techniques. His last job as makeup artist was on the TV show, *Mister Ed* (1961-1964) before dying in 1968 from kidney failure. He was one of the greatest pioneers of cinematic makeup in history.

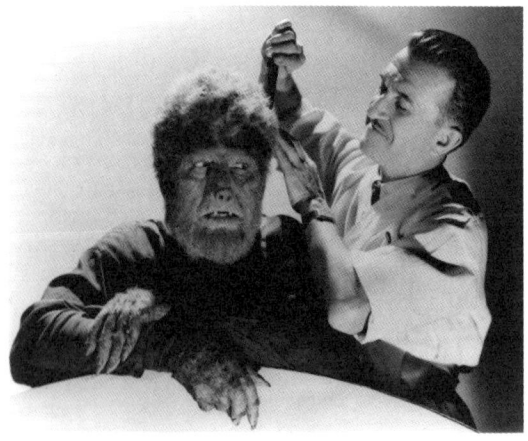

JOHN POLIDORI'S THE VAMPYRE

YES, THERE WERE VAMPIRES before *Dracula*. The image of the aristocratic fiend who preys among high society has a bloodline that predates Bram Stoker's famous story by nearly 80 years. John William Polidori was the chief physician of poet Lord Byron. While on a notorious weekend getaway with Byron and some now very famous guests, Polidori conceived the idea for *The Vampyre* (1819), based on a fragment of Byron's story about vampire myths in the Balkans. It centers on the exploits of a mysterious aristocrat named Lord Ruthven, who seduces and drains women of their blood. When he encounters a young English orphan named Aubrey, none of the women in Aubrey's life are safe. Upon initial publication the story was mistakenly attributed to Lord Byron, who later confirmed it belonged to his physician, Dr. Polidori. The vampire as we know it today was born here.

> *"Hell is just a frame of mind."*
> CHRISTOPHER MARLOWE (1564-1593), *Doctor Faustus*

WELCOME TO MY NIGHTMARE

After parting ways with the Alice Cooper band, singer and shock rocker Vincent Furnier teamed up with producer Bob Ezrin (Pink Floyd's *The Wall*) to take his notorious *Théâtre du Grand Guignol* stage theatrics up a notch on the writing level. The fruit of their labor was 1975's *Welcome to My Nightmare*, a concept record told from the perspective of a seven-year-old boy-turned serial killer named Steven, who's suffering some pretty serious nightmares among other mental wellness issues.

It is with this record that Vincent Furnier officially adopted the name Alice Cooper and fully embraced the character's penchant for twisted humor and horror. *Welcome to My Nightmare* explores themes of prostitution (*Devil's Food*); serial killing/rape (*The Black Widow*, featuring the vocal talents of Vincent Price); spousal abuse (*Only Women Bleed*) and even necrophilia (*Cold Ethyl*). The story is as eerie as it is morbidly funny—especially when supported by Cooper's outrageous live onstage theatrics, which typically include the singer hanging, decapitating, and otherwise mutilating himself.

Alice Cooper has had cameos in several horror films including John Carpenter's *Prince of Darkness* (1987), *Freddy's Dead: The Final Nightmare* (1991), *The Attic Expeditions* (2001), *Suck* (2009) and Tim Burton's reboot of *Dark Shadows* (2012).

13 SCARIEST HORROR VIDEO GAMES

Sometimes video games can be more frightening than movies, in part because players are directly immersed in them. Here are thirteen you should play with the lights off.

1	PENUMBRA: BLACK PLAGUE (2008, Frictional Games)
2	CONDEMNED: CRIMINAL ORIGINS (2005, Monolith Productions)
3	AMNESIA: THE DARK DESCENT (2010, Frictional Games)
4	ETERNAL DARKNESS: SANITY'S REQUIEM (2002, Silicon Knights)
5	F.E.A.R. (2005, Monolith Productions)
6	SILENT HILL 2 (2001, Konami)
7	DEAD SPACE (2008, EA Redwood Shores)
8	ALAN WAKE (2010, Remedy Entertainment)
9	RESIDENT EVIL 4 (2005, Capcom Production Studio 4)
10	BIOSHOCK (2005, Irrational Games)
11	LEFT 4 DEAD 2 (2009, Value Corporation/Turtle Rock Studios)
12	DOOM 3 (2004, id Software)
13	SLENDER: THE EIGHT PAGES (2012, Parsec Productions)

WHO GOES THERE?

FIRST PUBLISHED IN THE AUGUST 1938 issue of *Astounding Science-Fiction*, John W. Campbell Jr.'s *Who Goes There?* is a landmark science fiction novella that has been adapted three times as *The Thing from Another World* (1951), *The Thing* (1982), and its prequel, *The Thing* (2011). In the story, a group of scientific researchers discover a 20 million-year-old space ship buried in the ice of Antarctica. They unwisely thaw out its pilot, which immediately begins physically imitating the crew. *Who Goes There?* is a masterpiece of literature seething with paranoia, isolation, and cold, inescapable dread. It was best adapted in 1982 by John Carpenter with astounding special effects work by Rob Bottin. The film is often incorrectly identified as a remake of *The Thing from Another World* (1951), itself a loose adaptation of the story. Carpenter eschewed much of this version and went straight to the source material for his masterwork of apocalyptic internal invasion. Even the infamous "blood test" is straight from Campbell's novella. It remains the most faithful adaptation of the story to date.

PENNY DREADFULS

PRINTED ON CHEAP PULP PAPER and aimed at the British working class, "penny dreadfuls" (other known pejoratives: "penny horrible," "penny awful," "penny number," and "penny blood") were 19th century serialized tales of horror and sensational fiction, each costing a penny. They were the earliest form of pulp fiction, affordable alternatives to costly mainstream fiction. By 1850, most of the penny dreadfuls were aimed at adolescents. The stage equivalent was the "penny gaff." The most famous penny part-stories included Thomas Prest's *The Calendar of Horrors* (1835-1836), *Sweeny Todd* (first published as *The String of Pearls* in 1847), James Malcolm Rymer's *Varney the Vampire, or, the Feast of Blood* (1845) and George Reynolds' *Wagner the Werewolf* (1846). At the time, parents attributed all youth crime to the penny dreadfuls and swiftly banned and destroyed them. Comic books, "video nasties," and computer games would suffer similar accusations and intolerance many years later.

IT WAS A DARK AND STORMY NIGHT IN SWITZERLAND

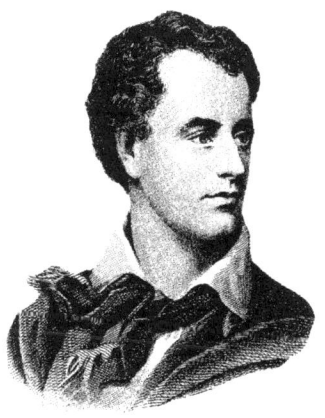

BETWEEN JUNE 15 AND 17, 1816, poet Lord Byron and his personal physician, Dr. John William Polidori, settled at Villa Diodati on Lake Geneva in Switzerland for the weekend. They were joined by guests Percy Bysshe Shelley, his fiancée Mary Wollstonecraft Godwin, and her stepsister Claire Clairmont—who was desperately in love with Byron. One stormy evening, after reading aloud stories from the popular horror anthology, *Tales of the Dead* (and possibly under the influence of laudanum), Byron challenged everyone to write a horror story. The result was the creation of the vampire and science fiction genres in English, thanks to Mary—who wrote a tale that evolved into *Frankenstein*—and Polidori—whose contribution became the first vampire tale in the English language. A number of films have depicted this literary lightning bolt of a weekend, including Ken Russell's *Gothic* (1986), Ivan Passer's *Haunted Summer* (1988), and Gonzalo Suárez's *Rowing with the Wind* (1988).

DOCTOR FAUSTUS

First printed posthumously in 1604, *The Tragical History of the Life and Death of Doctor Faustus* is the semi-autobiographical play about Johannes Faustus, a German scholar and magician who takes Mephistopheles as his servant for 24 years in exchange for his soul. Intensely demonic (or downright Satanic) for its time, Christopher Marlowe's *Doctor Faustus* raised much controversy and is considered to be the first dramatic adaptation of the Faust legend. It became the prototype for the mad scientist who sells his soul to the Devil in exchange for knowledge. Famously adapted by Goethe roughly 200 years later in 1808.

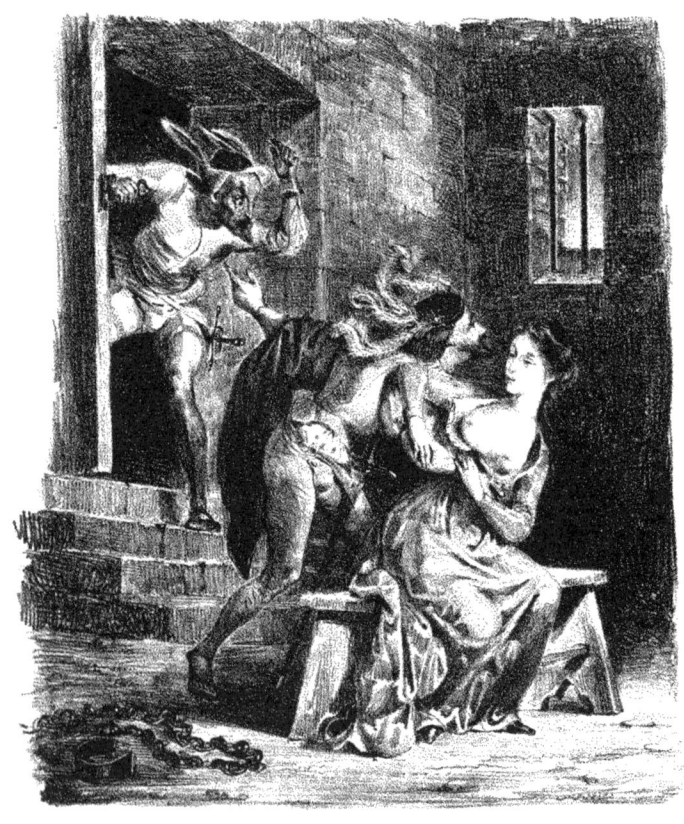

GODZILLA TRIVIA

Godzilla has become Japan's most widely recognized cultural icon—he even has a star on the Hollywood Walk of Fame at 6925 Hollywood Blvd.

Godzilla is 50 meters (164 feet) tall, *not* 400 feet, as stated in the edited American version.

Producer Tomoyuki Tanaka originally wanted Godzilla to be a giant fire-breathing ape (inspired by King Kong), and effects man Eiji Tsuburaya wanted Godzilla to be a giant octopus.

Godzilla was originally going to be portrayed via stop motion animation, but Eiji Tsuburaya abandoned the idea because of the cost and time associated. This is how the Godzilla rubber suit came to be.

The first Godzilla suit weighed 200 pounds. It was common for the crew to drain a cup of performer Haruo Nakajima's sweat from it.

Godzilla has appeared in 28 films produced by Toho Co., Ltd.

HELLBOY

CONJURED BY THE NAZIS on December 23, 1944, Hellboy is a demon that was born to murder the world. But before that happens, he is rescued by a shadowy international agency called the B.P.R.D. and brought up by humans to perform the opposite function: protection against things that go bump in the night. The unlikely superhero first appeared in *San Diego Comic-Con Comics* #2 (August, 1993) from creator Mike Mignola before going on to star in his own series at Dark Horse Comics. The eponymous title caught the attention of filmmaker Guillermo del Toro, who adapted the comic into two films *Hellboy* (2004) and *Hellboy II: The Golden Army* (2008), with Ron Perlman in the title role. The comic series is deeply rooted in world folklore, monsters, and Lovecraftian cosmic horror. The *Hellboy* universe has since expanded to animation, video games, role-playing games, and prose fiction.

> *"Libraries are filled with stories on generations of brutal men, trapped in a cycle of aggression. I wanted to write about the violence of women."*
> GILLIAN FLYNN (BORN 1971), *US author and critic*

GHOST STORIES OF AN ANTIQUARY

M.R. JAMES is widely regarded as one of the greatest practitioners of supernatural short fiction. His most important and well-known works are collected in *Ghost Stories of an Antiquary* (1904) and its sequel, *More Ghost Stories* (1911). These formally perfect stories focused on a series of historical objects (a scrapbook, a whistle, etc.), designed to be read aloud in the tradition of fireside Christmas Eve tales. Written with historical accuracy, suspense, and humor, James anticipated modern horror stories by placing his tales in a familiar settings. Jacques Tourneur's film, *Curse of the Demon* (1957) is based on one of James' best tales, *Casting the Runes*.

"YOU'RE GONNA NEED A BIGGER BOAT"

THIS IS IT, THE MOVIE THAT MADE an entire generation afraid to swim in the ocean, take a shower, or even wash their hands. Based on Peter Benchley's novel of the same name, *Jaws* (1975) tells the story of an enormous great white shark terrorizing the quaint island of Amity. In the hands of any other filmmaker, this flimsy monster movie premise could fall apart like a house of cards, but with a young and hungry Steven Spielberg at the helm, it was a blockbuster success. In a way, part of the film's brilliant suspense building is the result of serendipity. The special effects crew failed to fully test the mechanical shark, which wasn't working, before principal photography began. This left Spielberg in a precarious situation. He had to shoot something, so he shot a bunch of footage of the shark's POV in the water to create the illusion of the its presence in the film while the crew tried to get "Bruce" up and swimming. Combined with the famous theme by John Williams, the overall effect of the shark POV is astonishing—especially for a PG-13 horror film. The famous musical motif cues the audience to the shark's invisible menace, which makes those scenes much more frightening.

> *"Why should not a writer be permitted to make use of the levers of fear, terror and horror because some feeble soul here and there finds it more than it can bear? Shall there be no strong meat at table because there happen to be some guests there whose stomachs are weak, or who have spoiled their own digestions?"*
>
> E.T.A. HOFFMANN (1776-1822),
> *German author, composer, music critic, artist*

—ESSENTIAL TALES OF EDGAR ALLAN POE—

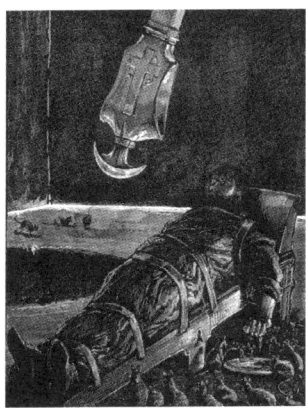

THE BLACK CAT (1843)

THE CASK OF AMONTILLADO (1846)

A DESCENT INTO THE MAELSTRÖM (1841)

THE FACTS IN THE CASE OF M. VALDEMAR (1845)

THE FALL OF THE HOUSE OF USHER (1839)

THE GOLD-BUG (1843)

HOP-FROG (1849)

THE IMP OF THE PERVERSE (1845)

LIGEIA (1838)

THE MASQUE OF THE RED DEATH (1842)

MORELLA (1835)

THE MURDERS IN THE RUE MORGUE (1841)

THE OVAL PORTRAIT (1842)

THE PIT AND THE PENDULUM (1842)

THE PREMATURE BURIAL (1844)

THE PURLOINED LETTER (1844)

THE SYSTEM OF DOCTOR TARR AND PROFESSOR FETHER (1845)

THE TELL-TALE HEART (1843)

J-HORROR

THE PHRASE HAS MOSTLY FALLEN out of fashion but "J-Horror" typically refers to the popular trend of Japanese horror films, beginning with 1998's *Ringu*, from director Hideo Nakata. The international success of *Ringu* launched a horror film production revival in Japan, which yielded some truly frightening supernatural films including Takashi Shimizu's *Ju-On* (2000), Kiyoshi Kurosawa's *Kairo* (2001), Nakata's *Dark Water* (2002), Higuchinsky's *Uzumaki* (2000) and the *Tomie* series (1999-2011).

Obviously, Japanese horror existed well before 1998, but *Ringu* helped bring the tradition of pallid long-haired ghost girls to the west—for better or worse. Mostly the latter, in the case of the remakes. Controversial filmmaking giant Takashi Miike (*Audition*) would be excluded from this area as he is in a league of his own.

KING OF GIMMICKS

WILLIAM CASTLE WAS AN AMERICAN FILM director and producer whose legendary showboating antics earned him the title, "King of Gimmicks." Castle was born William Schloss in New York City on April 24, 1914. He started tricking people early on. Posing as the nephew of Hollywood producer Samuel Goldwyn, the future master of ballyhoo got his start in film as an actor in Jules Leventhal's *An American Tragedy* (1931). Castle later charmed Orson Welles into letting him take over the Connecticut Theater in Stony Creek, where he'd devise his first professional gimmick: vandalizing his own theater with swastikas to promote his play, *Mädchen in Uniform* (1931).

Castle's debut as a director was the "Boston Blackie" mystery *The Chance of a Lifetime* (1943), which received dismal reviews. After seeing the French psychological thriller *Les Diaboliques* (1955), Castle became inspired to make horror films. His first outing, 1958's *Macabre*, was self-financed and shot in one week. Seeing the finished product, he decided he needed a gimmick to sell the film so he purchased a $5,000 life insurance policy from Lloyd's of London guaranteeing a $1,000 pay out to anyone who died of fright during the screening. And so began the illustrious career of Hollywood's greatest showman, whose gimmicks were often more entertaining than his films. Castle's most reputable credit is as a producer for *Rosemary's Baby* (1968).

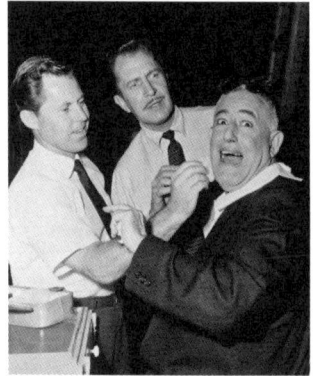

> "I became insane, with long intervals of horrible sanity. During these fits of absolute unconsciousness, I drank—God only knows how often or how much. As a matter of course, my enemies referred the insanity to the drink rather than the drink to the insanity. I had, indeed, nearly abandoned all hope of a permanent cure, when I found one in the death of my wife. This I can and do endure as becomes a man. It was the horrible never-ending oscillation between hope and despair which I could not longer have endured, without total loss of reason."
>
> EDGAR ALLAN POE (1809-1849) *US poet and author*

CASTLE'S GREATEST GIMMICKS

MACABRE (1958): A certificate for a $1,000 life insurance policy was given to each ticketholder in the event they die of fright and ambulatory care (nurses and hearses) was offered outside the theater.

THE TINGLER (1959): Filmed in "Percepto," *The Tingler* had audiences screaming for their lives as seats vibrated during the titular creature's attacks.

THE HOUSE ON HAUNTED HILL (1959): Filmed in Emergo! What was Emergo? A giant (goofy) inflatable skeleton on a wire that hovered over the audience during key scenes.

13 GHOSTS (1960): Illusion-O had viewers looking through colored cellophane cards to either see or not see the 13 phantoms in the film.

HOMICIDAL (1961): This gag included a 45-second "fright break" with an explanation that anyone too scared to go on could receive a refund and sit in "coward's corner" out in the lobby.

MR. SARDONICUS (1961): Audiences were allowed to vote and decide the fate of Mr. Sardonicus. Allegedly, no one ever chose to have the villain cured and that ending was never filmed.

STRAIGHT JACKET (1964): Castle had promised his financial backers he'd release this film without gimmicks, but couldn't help himself and had cardboard axes made to hand out to patrons at the last minute.

I SAW WHAT YOU DID (1965): Castle turned the back rows of theaters screening this film into "Shock Sections," equipped with seatbelts to keep patrons from bolting from their seats in fright.

BUG (1975): Castle advertised a $1,000,000 life insurance policy for the film's star, a cockroach named "Hercules."

HAMMER FILMS

PICKING UP WHERE UNIVERSAL LEFT OFF, British film studio Hammer became famous for recycling—albeit with more sex and violence—established horror icons in hundreds of films including *The Curse of Frankenstein* (1957), *Horror of Dracula* (1958), *The Mummy* (1959), *Curse of the Werewolf* (1961), and *The Phantom of the Opera* (1964). This hugely successful, and prolific, run of sexy Gothic thrillers cemented the company's reputation as the "Hammer House of Horror." The still-vital film company found renewed success recently with *The Woman in Black* (2012), starring Daniel Radcliffe.

TOP 15 CLASSIC HAMMER HORROR FILMS

THE QUATERMASS EXPERIMENT (dir. Val Guest, 1955)

THE CURSE OF FRANKENSTEIN (dir. Terence Fisher, 1957)

HORROR OF DRACULA (dir. Terence Fisher, 1958)

THE HOUND OF THE BASKERVILLES (dir. Terence Fisher, 1959)

THE GORGON (dir. Terence Fisher, 1964)

DRACULA, PRINCE OF DARKNESS (dir. Terence Fisher, 1966)

QUATERMASS AND THE PIT (dir. Roy Ward Baker, 1967)

DRACULA HAS RISEN FROM THE GRAVE (dir. Freddie Francis, 1968)

THE DEVIL RIDES OUT (dir. Terence Fisher, 1968)

FRANKENSTEIN MUST BE DESTROYED (dir. Terence Fisher, 1969)

THE VAMPIRE LOVERS (dir. Roy Ward Baker, 1970)

DR. JEKYLL AND SISTER HYDE (dir. Roy Ward Baker, 1971)

TWINS OF EVIL (dir. John Hough, 1971)

THE SATANIC RITES OF DRACULA (dir. Alan Gibson, 1973)

THE LEGEND OF THE 7 GOLDEN VAMPIRES (dir. Roy Ward Baker, 1974)

THE LAST HOUSE ON THE LEFT

LOOSELY BASED on Ingmar Bergman's *The Virgin Spring* (1960), *The Last House on the Left* (1972) is a grim "rape and revenge" movie and the first film from director Wes Craven. Mari and her friend Phyllis head to New York to see a concert when they are apprehended and brutally gang-raped and murdered by a group of very bad guys. Shot in a graphic and intense *cinéma vérité* style *à la* George Romero's *Night of the Living Dead*, *The Last House on the Left* has a perverse, abrasive home movie aesthetic that makes it difficult to watch. For all of its brutality and ugliness, *The Last House on the Left* is an important film in the evolution of American horror cinema. It marked the beginning of a new wave of uncompromising horror movies that depicted real-world horror. Craven went on to make the cannibal film, *The Hills Have Eyes* (1977), before finding mainstream success with *A Nightmare on Elm Street* (1984), and the meta-horror *Scream* franchise (1996-2011). *The Last House on the Left* was unsurprisingly remade, to lesser effect, in 2009.

DANSE MACABRE

DEATH IS UNIVERSAL. NO MATTER one's station in life, the Dance of Death unites all. That is the meaning behind "Danse Macabre" or "Dance of Death," a popular late-medieval allegory about death and dying. There have been many depictions; the most popular include Brueghel's masterful, *The Triumph of Death* and a German woodcut, thought to be created by Michael Wolgemut (1434-1519), in which Death summons people from all walks of life to the grave. The earliest recorded visual depiction of the "Danse Macabre" was a mural in The Saints Innocents Cemetery in Paris, France (1424-1425), now lost. The first edition of the *Danse Macabre* poem, with illustrations inspired by the French mural was published in Paris in 1485 by Guyot Marchant.

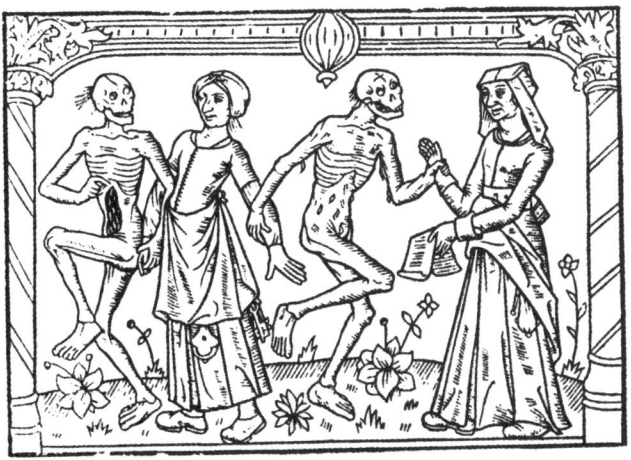

ARKHAM HOUSE

THE ARKHAM HOUSE PUBLISHING COMPANY was founded in 1939 in Sauk City, Wisconsin by August Derleth and Donald Wandrei in an effort to preserve the fictional work and letters of H.P. Lovecraft. The company's name is derived from the author's fictional New England city. It's known for its high quality hardcover editions of Lovecraft's material, reprints of classic horror fiction, and titles by Ray Bradbury, Robert Bloch, Robert E. Howard, and Clark Ashton Smith. The company still publishes "weird fiction" (albeit irregularly) to this day.

EDISON'S FRANKENSTEIN

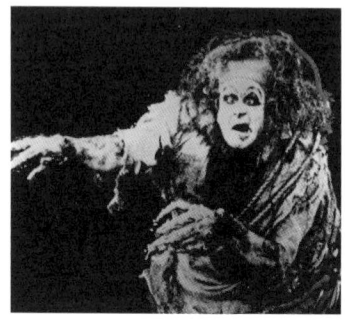

THE FIRST motion picture adaptation of Mary Shelley's *Frankenstein* arrived in 1910 with J. Searle Dawley's *Frankenstein*, a 16-minute one-reel short made for Edison Studios. A film of enormous historical importance to the horror genre, it is widely considered the first American horror film, though the studio intended to downplay the horrific elements of Shelley's weird tale. Unlike other versions of the story, Doctor Frankenstein (Augustus Phillips) creates his monster (played by Charles Ogle, looking like a demented, fat court jester) in a metal vat from mystical potions, as opposed to assembled parts fused together through science fiction. The monster escapes its barricaded birthing room and tries to comfort its grief stricken creator and even follows him home like a loyal dog. The monster never seeks vengeance, nor does it commit any acts of violence or murder. Upon seeing its own reflection in a mirror, it fades away and only Dr. Frankenstein remains, reminiscent of *Dr. Jekyll and Mr. Hyde*. It was thought lost until its rediscovery in the archive of Wisconsin film collector Alois F. Dettlaff in the 1970s.

TOP TEN MONSTROUS MOVIE MATRIARCHS

1	Margaret White, *Carrie* (dir. Brian De Palma, 1976)
2	Vera Cosgrove (AKA Mum), *Dead Alive* (dir. Peter Jackson. 1992)
3	Nola Carveth, *The Brood* (dir. David Cronenberg, 1979)
4	Mrs. Norma Bates, *Psycho* (dir. Alfred Hitchcock, 1960)
5	Mrs. Rand, *I Walked with a Zombie* (dir. Jacques Tourneur, 1943)
6	The Women, *Onibaba* (dir. Kaneto Shindô, 1964)
7	Pamela Voorhees, *Friday the 13TH* (dir. Sean S. Cunningham, 1980)
8	Kayako, *Ju-On* (dir. Takashi Shimizu, 2002)
9	Alien Queen, *Aliens* (dir. James Cameron, 1986)
10	Joan Crawford, *Mommie Dearest* (dir. Frank Perry, 1981)

BODY COUNT BY HORROR FILM

1	GRINDHOUSE: DOUBLE FEATURE (dir. Robert Rodriguez and Quentin Tarrentino, 2007)	310
2	DAWN OF THE DEAD (dir. George A. Romero, 1978)	175
3	HOUSE OF THE DEAD (dir. Uwe Boll, 2003)	141
4	DAWN OF THE DEAD (dir. Zack Snyder, 2004)	131
5	RESIDENT EVIL: EXTINCTION (dir. Paul W.S. Anderson, 2007)	124
6	RESIDENT EVIL: APOCALYPSE (dir. Paul W.S. Anderson, 2004)	123
7	ALIENS VS. PREDATOR: REQUIEM (dir. Colin and Greg Strause, 2007)	115
8	ARMY OF DARKNESS (dir. Sam Raimi, 1993)	107
9	BLOODRAYNE (dir. Uwe Boll, 2005)	102
10	PREDATOR (dir. John McTiernan, 1987)	64

source: moviebodycounts.com

MONDO CANE

A KEY PRECURSOR TO THE MONDO subgenre, as well as the cannibal film, *Mondo Cane* (AKA *A Dog's World*) is the mother of all exploitation shockumentaries. In fact, the entire contemporary found footage or "shaky cam" horror film subgenre can be traced all the way back to 1962's *Mondo Cane*.

Italian filmmakers Paolo Cavara, Gualtiero Jacopetti, and Franco Prosperi compiled a collection of unrelated archival footage of humankind behaving badly—"barbarians" engaging in bizarre rituals, "savages" committing animal cruelty—from around the world, edited it with staged footage and presented it as a quasi-documentary. Make no mistake, this is white male ethnocentrism at its worst. Despite its flimsy claim of objective authenticity and disreputable content, *Mondo Cane* became a tremendous box office success. It even got an Oscar nomination for the theme song, *More*, by composers Riz Ortolani and Nino Oliviero.

This real-or-not shockumentary conceit inspired many sequels and spin-offs, which include other culturally denigrating films such as *Africa Addio* and *Shocking Asia*. It would also be repurposed and reinvented famously by Ruggero Deodato in *Cannibal Holocaust* (1980), and the notorious *Faces of Death* films. The Mondo esthetic lives on in supposed "found footage" horror films including *The Blair Witch Project* (1999) and the enormously successful *Paranormal Activity* (2007-2013) franchise.

GERMAN EXPRESSIONISM

AROUND 1905, A MULTIDISCIPLINARY artistic movement known as Expressionism began to emerge in Germany. A modernist movement that originated in poetry and painting, Expressionism was a direct rejection of the naturalist values inherent in Impressionism. Instead, it embraced primitivism, producing a more symbolic and abstract mode of artistic expression that came from within the artist himself. It's a difficult movement to categorize, but it's safe to say Expressionist Art often portrayed an individual perspective, particularly emotional and psychological. Expressionism's influence was far reaching, taken up in music, theater, literature, painting, sculpture, architecture, and finally, film.

The first Expressionist films (known as "Kammerspielfilm") were created between the great World Wars. These films are characterized by an intense, high contrast visual style and fantastic subject matter including artificial creatures, Faustian bargains, and doppelgangers. Emphasis was on design, *mise-en-scène*, uncanny atmosphere, and composition. Today German Expressionism is used a blanket term for all chiaroscuro films from the period and region, but the movement had a blurry beginning, middle, and end. Traces begin to appear as early as *The Student of Prague* (1913) and most definitely do not extend beyond Fritz Lang's *Metropolis* (1927), and *M* (1931). Films such as *Nosferatu* (1922) and *Der Golem* (1920) are often lumped into this category, but are not purist German Expressionist films. In fact, directors F.W. Murnau and Paul Wegener rejected the label outright, insisting their films were more informed by naturalism.

The movement peaked with Robert Wiene's *Das Cabinet des Dr. Caligari* (1920), a seminal horror film that would have an immense influence on the look of later Hollywood films including the Universal Monster cycle and the film noir genre. In it, elaborate, distorted sets were designed to express the distorted view of the film's central figure, a madman named Caligari. *Caligari* was a resounding success in the United States, where Hollywood took an interest. Filmmakers (Paul Leni and Murnau among them), actors (including Conrad Veidt), and cameramen (Karl Freund) were lured to California, where they would have a profound influence on the progression of horror cinema.

> "The Devil pulls the strings which make us dance;
> We find delight in the most loathsome things;
> Some furtherance of Hell each new day brings,
> And yet we feel no horror in that rank advance."
> CHARLES BAUDELAIRE (1821-1867), *To the Reader*

DRACULA TRIVIA

The working titles for *Dracula* were *The Dead Un-Dead* and *The Un-Dead*.

The original name of the villain was "Count Wampyr." Stoker came across the name Vlad Dracula (Vlad the Impaler) while researching Romanian history.

The name Dracula means "Son of Dracul." Dracul mean "dragon" or "devil."

Stoker had a day job as a manager for actor Sir Henry Irving, whom he based Count Dracula's "psychic vampire" persona and dramatic gesticulations on.

The first cinematic adaptation of *Dracula* was in 1921, with *Drakula*, a Hungarian film that no longer exists.

Francis Ford Coppola's 1992 *Dracula* is the only film adaptation that depicts the vampire crawling down the outside of the castle, as described in the original text.

In the cinema, the character of Dracula has appeared in well over 200 films over the last 90 years.

Dracula is not the first vampire novel. It is preceded by Sheridan Le Fanu's *Carmilla* (1871), James Malcolm Rymer's *Varney the Vampire* (1845-47), John Polidori's *The Vampyre*, and Johann Ludwig Tieck's *Wake Not the Dead*.

PETER JACKSON

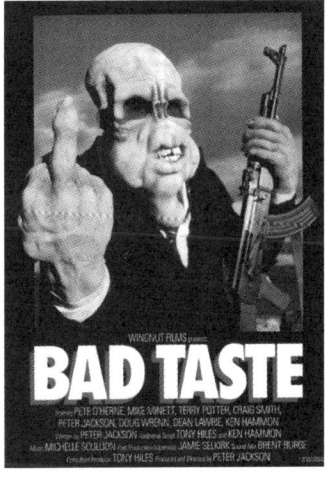

Before becoming a blockbuster film director, Academy Award-winning filmmaker Peter Jackson was known in the indie horror scene as a splatter comedy king. If you only know Peter Jackson from *The Lord of the Rings* franchise and his take on *King Kong* (2005), please close this book and watch the following films: *Bad Taste* (1987), *Meet the Feebles* (1989), *Braindead* AKA *Dead Alive* (1992), and *The Frighteners* (1996). Here, you will find the filmmaker at his bravest and most idiosyncratic.

NACHTSTÜCKE

ERNST THEODOR Amadeus Hoffmann (1776-1822), better known by his pen name E. T. A. Hoffmann, was a German Romantic author of fantasy and horror. *Nachtstücke* (*"The Night Pieces"*), Hoffman's 1817 anthology of uncanny tales includes *Tale of the Lost Shadow* and notably, *The Sandman*, a haunting depiction of madness that was extensively interpreted by Sigmund Freud in his famous 1919 essay, *The Uncanny*. According to Freud, the Uncanny is "the opposite of what is familiar" and is "frightening precisely because it is not known and familiar." He calls Hoffmann "a master of the uncanny," who was a major influence on the German Expressionists of the early 20th century.

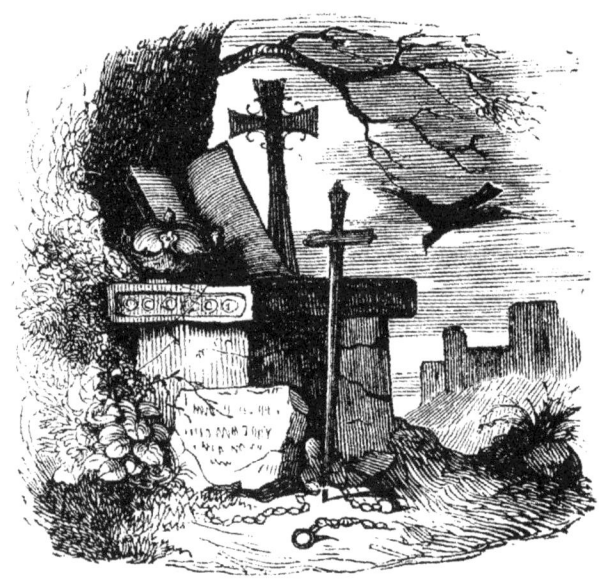

> "I shall never permit anything bearing my signature to be banalised and vulgarised into the flat, infantile twaddle which passes for 'horror tales' amongst radio and cinema audiences."
> H.P. LOVECRAFT (1890-1937), *US writer and editor*

10 MOST CHILLING TWILIGHT ZONE EPISODES

1. THE EYE OF THE BEHOLDER (Season 2)
2. THE MONSTERS ARE DUE ON MAPLE STREET (Season 1)
3. TO SERVE MAN (Season 3)
4. TIME ENOUGH AT LAST (Season 1)
5. NIGHTMARE AT 20,000 FEET (Season 5)
6. WILL THE REAL MARTIAN PLEASE STAND UP? (Season 2)
7. IT'S A GOOD LIFE (Season 3)
8. STOPOVER IN A QUIET TOWN (Season 1)
9. LIVING DOLL (Season 5)
10. THE INVADERS (Season 2)

GHOSTS'N GOBLINS

A HUGE WINGED DEMON has kidnapped Princess Guinevere, and the only person who can rescue her from his clawed clutches is you! Playing as Prince Arthur, gamers in 1985 immersed themselves in this horror-themed upright arcade game from Capcom, fighting hordes of zombies, demons, cyclops, dragons, and other monsters, while wearing a rather flimsy suit of armor. It begins in a graveyard and ends in an epic battle with Satan. What more could you ask for in a horror experience? Despite being one of the most notoriously difficult platform games in existence, *Ghosts'n Goblins* was a huge hit and has been retrofitted to many game platforms ever since.

GILLIAN FLYNN

GILLIAN FLYNN WRITES THRILLERS. Really dark, twisted thrillers. A former television critic for *Entertainment Weekly*, Flynn left her post to explore the violence of women in three best-selling novels: *Sharp Objects* (2006), *Dark Places* (2009), and *Gone Girl* (2012). Her books are the literary equivalent of a chick flick for the horror set. She writes psychopaths and broken people as well as Thomas Harris, and crafts mystery and suspense as finely as Alfred Hitchcock.

A GOTHIC HORROR READER: THE SECOND WAVE

THE LIVING CORPSE—Vladimir Odoevsky (1844)
VARNEY THE VAMPIRE OR THE FEAST OF BLOOD—James Malcolm Rymer/Thomas Peckett Prest (1847)
LES CHANTS DE MALDOROR—Comte de Lautréamont (1869)
CARMILLA—Sheridan Le Fanu (1872)
IN A GLASS DARKLY—Sheridan Le Fanu (1872)
THE STRANGE CASE OF DR. JEKYLL AND MR. HYDE—Robert Louis Stevenson (1885)
THE HORLA—Guy de Maupassant (1887)
THE PICTURE OF DORIAN GRAY—Oscar Wilde (1890)
THE YELLOW WALLPAPER—Charlotte Perkins Gilman (1892)
THE BLACK MONK—Anton Pavlovich Chekhov (1894)
THE KING IN YELLOW—Robert W. Chambers (1895)
DRACULA—Bram Stoker (1897)
THE TURN OF THE SCREW—Henry James (1898)
THE MONKEY'S PAW—W. W. Jacobs (1902)
THE HOUSE ON THE BORDERLAND—William Hope Hodgson (1907)
THE PHANTOM OF THE OPERA—Gaston Leroux (1910)

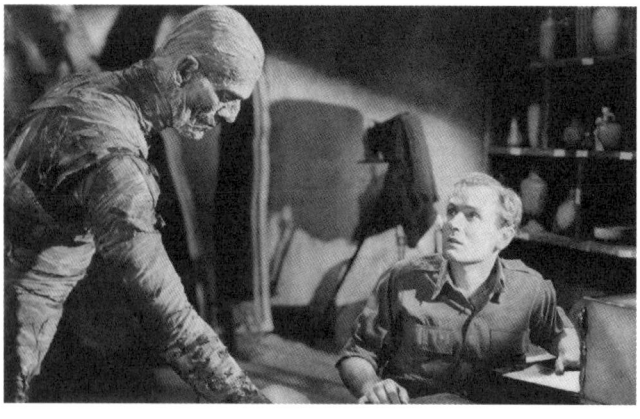

MISFITS

Formed in Lodi, New Jersey in 1977 by singer Glenn Danzig, The Misfits are horror punk's original monster squad. Despite ongoing line-up changes, Danzig and guitarist Jerry Only released several EPs and singles that were heavily inspired by B-horror and sci-fi films including, *Night of the Living Dead* and *Horror Business*. Bedecked in dark clothes with skeletal patterns, "devil lock" hairstyles, and ghoulish make-up, The Misfits toured the burgeoning hardcore punk nightclub scene playing their own brand of horror-obsessed, primitive-punk-rock-meets-1950s-style-rock-and-roll.

Their first studio album, *Static Age*, was recorded in 1978, but wasn't released until 1997 on their label, Plan 9 Records (named after the infamously inept Ed Wood film). The Misfits then recorded *Walk Among Us* (1982) and *Earth A.D./Wolf's Blood* (1983) before disbanding in 1983, with Danzig going on to form Samhain and eventually his eponymous solo project, Danzig.

After a decade-long legal battle, The Misfits reformed in 1985 without Danzig. Jerry Only and his brother, Doyle Wolfgang Von Frankenstein, released the heavy metal albums *American Psycho* in 1997 and *Famous Monsters* (named after the beloved horror magazine) in 1999, with singer Michale Graves. Both records were heavily steeped in horror, featuring songs such as *Abominable Dr. Phibes*, *Mars Attacks*, *Crawling Eye*, and *Pumpkin Head*. The music video for *Scream!* was even directed by George A. Romero (*Dawn of the Dead*), who worked for free in exchange for the use of two Misfits songs in his 1993 film *Bruiser*. In 2001, Only took over singing duties and became the sole original remaining member of The Misfits. Their album, *The Devil's Rain* (2011), is named after the 1971 horror film.

The Misfits still tour the globe relentlessly, picking up new fans along the way. The band's original "fiend club" fan club, started by Danzig as a D-I-Y operation, has transcended generations and evolved into a full-fledged merchandising machine. The easily recognizable "Fiend Skull" mascot is inspired by a poster for the 1946 film serial, *The Crimson Ghost*. It appeared for the fist time on the 1979 *Horror Business* single, and can be seen on the backs of teenagers all over the world today. Bands such as Metallica, Guns 'n' Roses, Slayer, Pantera, Marilyn Manson, and Rob Zombie all cite The Misfits as an inspiration for their music.

> *"I do know that for the sympathy of one living being, I would make peace with all. I have love in me the likes of which you can scarcely imagine and rage the likes of which you would not believe. If I cannot satisfy the one, I will indulge the other."*
> MARY SHELLEY (1797-1851), *Frankenstein*

5 INDISPENSIBLE BLACK AND WHITE HORROR FILMS

1 NIGHT OF THE HUNTER (1955)—Actor Charles Laughton steps behind the camera for the first and last time to direct this masterpiece starring Robert Mitchum as a charlatan preacher who terrorizes a widow and her children in pursuit of their father's hidden money. There's nothing quite like this suspenseful, Expressionist southern Gothic thriller.

2 ONIBABA (1964)—This black and white Japanese film is a masterpiece. Desperate women lure Samurai soldiers to their deaths in Kaneto Shindô's take on the classic Japanese folk tale of female jealousy and rage.

3 THE HOUR OF THE WOLF (1968)—Ingmar Bergman is most well known for his stunning allegory of man's search for meaning in *The Seventh Seal*, but it is his only horror film, *The Hour of the Wolf*, that is utterly captivating in its depiction of an artist's loss of sanity. Depressing and nightmarish, like all good horror films should be.

4 THE INNOCENTS (1963)—Forget *The Others* (2001) and track down a copy of *The Innocents*, the original haunted heiress movie. It operates on the same level as *The Haunting* (1963) and *Rosemary's Baby* (1968), asking the viewer to figure out what is really going on. The chill of this film sets in like a winter fog, slow and quiet.

5 VAMPYR (1932)—Subtitled *The Dream of Allen Gray*, Carl Theodor Dreyer's oneiric vampire film (based on *Carmilla* by Sheridan Le Fanu) details the experiences of a occult-obsessed traveler who is caught up in a maddening nightmare when he beds down at a French inn that is under the grip of a vampire. *Vampyr* eschews narrative logic in favour of poetic visuals and eerie sound design—all culminating in an overbearing sense of dread. Unconventional, moody and menacing, it's easy to see the influence of *Vampyr* on filmmakers such as Jess Franco and David Lynch.

THE REAL FIRST VAMPIRE STORY

WRITTEN BY JOHANN LUDWIG TIECK, *Wake Not the Dead* (1800) is considered the first fictional vampire story ever written—in German. It was not translated into English until 1823, four years after the publication of John Polidori's *The Vampyre*. Nevertheless, *Wake Not the Dead* remains the first modern vampire romance—about a man who so cannot bear the death of his wife that he has her resurrected by a necromancer, only to find out she has become a vampire. In the end he must destroy her and pay the price for not heeding the warning: "Wake Not the Dead." Words to live by.

THE UNIVERSAL MONSTERS LEGACY

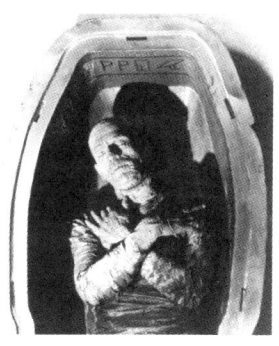

UNIVERSAL STUDIOS WAS THE BIRTHPLACE of horror in America. It all began with 1923's *The Hunchback of Notre Dame*, starring Lon Chaney—a special effects practitioner willing to go to great lengths to pull off a character. The historical drama was such a financial and critical success, it inspired the studio to produce its first bona fide horror film: 1925's *The Phantom of the Opera*, also starring Chaney. This was just the beginning of a tidal wave of horror films from the studio that didn't end until 1960.

Of course, the studio had its ups and downs. By the 1930s, silent films were declining and being replaced by "talkies." Universal's biggest star, Lon Chaney, had died and the studio was gasping for air. To its rescue came Tod Browning, and his adaptation of Bram Stoker's famous book, *Dracula* (1931). The film starred Hungarian born actor Bela Lugosi, a natural fit for an Eastern European aristocratic count. Though he was not the studio's first choice, Lugosi was fresh off a highly successful theatrical run of the *Dracula* play, which Universal purchased the rights to in 1930. Hazy cinematography from German Expressionist Karl Freund gave the film an otherworldly quality that audiences were captivated by. Lugosi went on to become one of the studio's biggest stars, alongside English born actor Boris Karloff, who starred in Universal's next horror film: *Frankenstein* (1931), directed by James Whale.

Lugosi was make-up tested for the role of Frankenstein's monster, but wasn't pleased to be hidden beneath make-up and have so few lines of dialogue. Hubris eventually turned to jealousy when *Frankenstein*, starring Karloff, went on to become even more successful than *Dracula*. The success of these two films allowed the studio to survive and encouraged the production of a series of monster movies that would bring us some of cinema's most memorable monsters including The Mummy, The Invisible Man, The Wolf Man, and The Bride of Frankenstein.

> *"We make up horrors to help us cope with the real ones."*
> STEPHEN KING (BORN 1947),
> *US author, film director, screenwriter, producer, actor*

THE EXORCIST

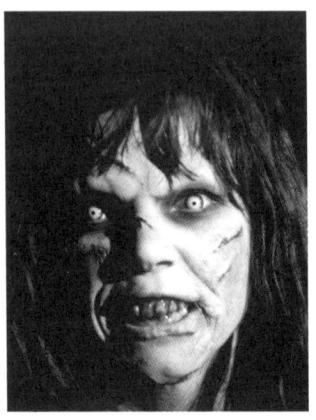

WILLIAM FRIEDKIN'S *The Exorcist* (1973) was the first horror film to be nominated for Best Picture, and deservedly so. Traditional as it may be, in its broad characterizations of good and evil, *The Exorcist* is one of the most frightening horror movies ever made. The film is based on the bestselling 1971 book by William Peter Blatty, which itself is inspired by the 1949 supposed exorcism case of Roland Doe.

In the film, a 12-year-old girl named Regan (Linda Blair) is possessed by a demonic entity called Pazuzu. After a series of medical tests that offer no explanation for her bizarre behavior, her distraught mother calls in a Jesuit priest, Father Damien Karras (Jason Miller), who is having a crisis of faith following the death of his mother. The ensuing exorcism performed by Karras and his elder, Father Lankester Merrin (Max Von Sydow), is one of the most memorable (and spoofed) sequences in cinema history. Features include Regan's head spinning completely around, projectile green vomit, and some truly horrifying make-ups by the legendary Dick Smith.

Despite its crucifix masturbation scene and general tone of horrific child abuse, *The Exorcist* ended up winning Oscars for Best Sound and Best Screenplay, and went on to become one of the top 10 highest grossing films of all time, scaring the pants off of millions of Devil-fearing people at the height of pre-millennial angst. It went on to inspire a host of foreign imitations and Stateside Devil movies including *The Sentinel* (1977) and *The Omen* films. After a period of dormancy, the exorcism subgenre returned with a spate of largely unoriginal Devil-themed movies including *The Rite* (2011), *The Exorcism of Emily Rose* (2005), *The Devil Inside* (2012), and *The Last Exorcism* (2010)—but none will ever hold a candle to Friedkin's chilling original.

> "Imagination, of course, can open any door—turn the key and let terror walk right in."
> TRUMAN CAPOTE (1924–1984), *In Cold Blood*

D.W. GRIFFITH'S EDGAR ALLAN POE

D.W. GRIFFITH's *Edgar Allan Poe* (1909) was one of Biograph's earliest shorts. This six-minute film draws from the life of the famously troubled eponymous author, who is seen being rejected by publishers as his wife ails and eventually dies moments before he returns with food and medicine. While not his finest work, Griffith did a remarkable job casting, as actor Herbert Yost bears a striking resemblance to Poe.

ANOTHER 10 GREAT HORROR SEQUELS

1 A NIGHTMARE ON ELM STREET 3: DREAM WARRIORS (dir. Chuck Russell, 1987): Easily the best of the sequels, starring Patricia Arquette and Laurence Fishburne.

2 ALIENS (dir. James Cameron, 1987): This high action sequel features plenty of guns, spaceships, monsters, and Sigourney Weaver kicking alien mother ass in a big mecha suit.

3 EVIL DEAD II (dir. Sam Raimi, 1987): Raimi's splatstick remake of his own film turned Michigander Bruce Campbell into a cult icon.

4 DAWN OF THE DEAD (dir. George Romero, 1978): There's a reason why this movie is on nearly every horror fan's all-time favorite list—it's original, scary, and subversive.

5 THE SILENCE OF THE LAMBS (dir. Jonathan Demme, 1991): The events in this Academy Award-winning adaptation of Thomas Harris' novel occur after the action in Michael Mann's superb film *Manhunter* (1986), making it sort of a sequel. And a damned good one.

6 INFERNO (dir. Dario Argento, 1980): Argento's weird and wonderful pseudo-sequel to *Suspiria*.

7 DAMIEN: OMEN II (dir. Don Taylor, 1978): Ever wondered what happened to the baby antichrist? He's a teenager! Excellent death scenes.

8 ALIEN³ (dir. David Fincher, 1992): If you've never seen the director's cut, you're missing out on a completely different and totally compelling film.

9 FRIDAY THE 13TH PART 2 (dir. Steve Miner, 1981): Jason Voorhees picks up where his mother left off after she was beheaded—sans mask.

10 NEW NIGHTMARE (dir. Wes Craven, 1994): Before *Scream*, Craven tackled meta-horror in the seventh entry of the *Elm Street* franchise. An interesting curio.

FRIDAY THE 13TH

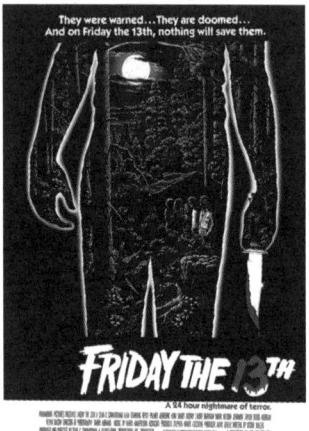

THEY SAY THE ROAD TO HELL is paved with good intentions. Seeking to distance himself from the nastiness of *The Last House on the Left* (1972), Sean Cunningham set out to make frightening horror film that was also fun. *Friday the 13TH* (1980) was inspired by John Carpenter's *Halloween* (1978) and, like most '80s slasher flicks, cribs heavily from Mario Bava's *A Bay of Blood* (1971).

The film was shot on a still-working New Jersey Boy Scout camp called Camp No-Be-Bo-Sco. Composer Harry Manfredini created a musical motif in the vein of *Jaws* that signaled the presence of the killer even though she was off-screen. The resulting "ki ki ki, ma ma ma" sound became an iconic motif in the *Friday the 13TH* franchise. The film was a huge box office success and helped usher the grubby grindhouse slasher film into the mainstream, spawning nine sequels, a crossover film with the *A Nightmare on Elm Street* franchise and a downright awful 2009 reboot. Although the character of Jason Voorhees was introduced in *Friday the 13TH: Part 2*, it was not until the third installment that he put on his trademark hockey mask.

INTERVIEW WITH THE VAMPIRE

IN THE LATE 1960S, author Anne Rice wrote a short story about a reporter who interviews a vampire that regales him with a tale of a once vibrant community of vampires. In 1973, while mourning the death of her five-year-old daughter to leukemia, Rice fleshed the short out to a 338-page gothic horror story that asks readers to identify with pained, philosophizing Victorian vampires, rather than their victims. *Interview with the Vampire* was published in May of 1977 and became a national bestseller. The book was succeeded by two sequels, *The Vampire Lestat* (1985), and *The Queen of the Damned* (1988) and was made into a major motion picture starring Brad Pitt and Tom Cruise in 1994.

JACK THE RIPPER

11 GRISLY MURDERS occurred in London's impoverished Whitechapel district between April 3, 1888 and February 13, 1891. Police received hundreds of letters from people claiming to be the killer. One was signed "Jack the Ripper," which when released to journalists caused an international media frenzy, thus giving birth to one of the most infamous and ubiquitous killers in history. Five of the murders, known as "the canonical five", were attributed to Jack the Ripper by London Police. The victims, all prostitutes, had their throats slashed prior to abdominal evisceration and genital mutilation. The skill at which some of the organs were excised led to speculation that The Ripper may have had surgical background. Others speculated butchers, slaughterers, royalty and all points in between. The case was never solved and Jack the Ripper remains unidentified; in fact, new suspects are still being "identified" every day. One thing's for certain: we'll never know who committed those crimes. The character, depicted in a cloak and top hat, has appeared in hundreds of works of fiction and the crimes are the subject of obsessive study by amateur "Ripperologists" worldwide.

A GERMAN EXPRESSIONIST FILM PRIMER

THE STUDENT OF PRAGUE (dir. Stellan Rye and Paul Wegener, 1913)

HOMUNCULUS (dir. Otto Rippert, 1916)

ALRAUNE (dir. Michael Curtiz and Edmund Fritz, 1918)

GENUINE (dir. Robert Wiene, 1920)

THE GOLEM (dir. Carl Boese and Paul Wegener, 1920)

THE HEAD OF JANUS (dir. F.W. Murnau, 1920)

DESTINY/THE WEARY DEATH (dir. Fritz Lang, 1921)

THE PHANTOM CARRIAGE (dir. Victor Sjöström, 1921)

FROM MORN TO MIDNIGHT (dir. Karl Heinz Martin, 1922)

PHANTOM (dir. F.W. Murnau, 1922)

RASKOLNIKOV (dir. Robert Wiene, 1923)

WARNING SHADOWS (dir. Arthur Robison, 1923)

THE LAST LAUGH (dir. F.W. Murnau, 1924)

WAXWORKS (dir. Leo Birinsky and Paul Leni, 1924)

FAUST (dir. F.W. Murnau, 1926)

IN THE MOUTH OF MADNESS

In the '80s and '90s, New Line Cinema was considered the home for horror movies. The distributor released more genre films during that two-decade span than any other—perhaps because its bosses were horror fans themselves. Producer and screenwriter Michael De Luca was president of production at New Line in 1988 when he penned a screenplay inspired by the weird fiction of American author H.P. Lovecraft. De Luca had been courting Carpenter to direct the film, entitled *In the Mouth of Madness*, and when director Mary Lambert (*Pet Sematary*) dropped out, Carpenter finally stepped in.

An insurance investigator, Trent (played by Sam Neill), is hired by the head of Arcane Publishing to investigate the disappearance of a popular horror novelist named Sutter Kane (played by Jurgen Prochnow in an obvious nod to Carpenter's friend and literary giant Stephen King). All signs point to Hobb's End, the fictional setting of many of Cane's stories. Convinced it's an elaborate publicity stunt to promote Cane's new book, Trent travels to Hobb's End, accompanied by Cane's editor, Linda Styles (Julie Carmen).

Upon their arrival they encounter many of the fictional characters and places from Cane's imagination including Pickman's Inn—where they stay—as well as the Black Church, where Cane has been hiding out. It becomes apparent that Cane's stories have unleashed an ancient evil that is slowly poisoning the town and turning its residents into mutated monsters and that his latest manuscript, *In the Mouth of Madness*, has the power to destroy the world. When Trent tries to escape, he is confronted with the jarring realization that Linda never existed, that he is a fictional character in Cane's story and, worse, that the apocalypse cannot be prevented.

The film is the third installment in what Carpenter calls his "Apocalypse Trilogy," which includes *The Thing* (1982) and *Prince of Darkness* (1987). In fact, he says it could even be perceived as a loose sequel to *Prince of Darkness*. While not a straight adaptation of H.P. Lovecraft, the film pays tribute to many of the author's works with references to several of his tales. The title is a play on two stories: *The Shadow Over Innsmouth* and *At the Mountains of Madness*. The character of Ms. Pickman is a nod to the short story *Pickman's Model* and Cane's book *The Hobb's End Horror* is a direct reference to *The Dunwich Horror*. Lovecraft's iconic "Old Ones" are mentioned briefly and the excerpt Cane reads aloud from his book is in fact borrowed directly from *The Outsider*, a poetic short about a narrator who discovers he is the stuff of his own nightmares. Finally, the overall theme of madness and bodily transmogrification as induced by interdimensional beings is pure Lovecraft.

COFFIN JOE

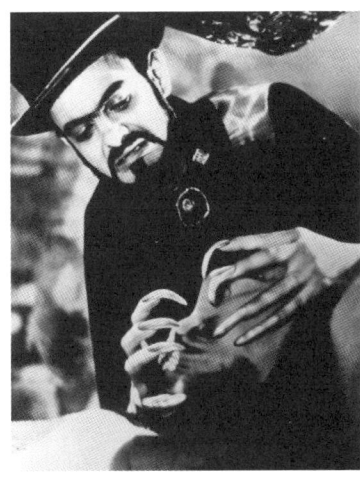

ZÉ DO CAIXÃO (roughly translated as "Coffin Joe") is Brazil's greatest boogeyman. He is the alter ego of José Mojica Marins, an actor/director/producer who dabbled in westerns, adventure, exploitation, softcore and, of course, horror films. Marins invented the character of Coffin Joe for *At Midnight I'll Take Your Soul* (1964), Brazil's first horror film.

An unholy undertaker and evil philosopher, Coffin Joe traipses around in a top hat and cape like some Brazilian Jack the Ripper with three-inch fingernails, blaspheming and terrorizing São Paulo locals. In a reach for immortality, he spends most of his time in the singular pursuit of preserving his bloodline, which he does by any means necessary, including kidnapping, rape, and murder. Coffin Joe has appeared as a central character in a trilogy of wholly original low budget films that include, *At Midnight I'll Take Your Soul* (1964), *This Night I'll Possess Your Corpse* (1967), and *Embodiment of Evil* (2008). These movies are characterized by misogyny, exploitation elements, and Coffin Joe's overtly anti-Christian antics. Despite Joe's misanthropic leanings, the character has become a pop culture icon in Brazil—like Elvira, but nastier and more nationally beloved.

THE KING IN YELLOW

ROBERT W. CHAMBERS' SUPERB 1895 COLLECTION of 10 supernatural stories had a direct influence on H.P. Lovecraft. Four of the short stories in the collection make mention of a fictional play entitled, *The King in Yellow*, a forbidden play that induces madness. Lovecraft read the collection in 1927 and borrowed the motif for his own writings in the Cthulhu mythos, which includes a forbidden but recurring fictional grimoire called *The Necronomicon* that—what else?—induces madness. He also makes references to things and places from *The King in Yellow* in *The Whisperer in the Darkness* (1931).

PLANET OF THE VAMPIRES

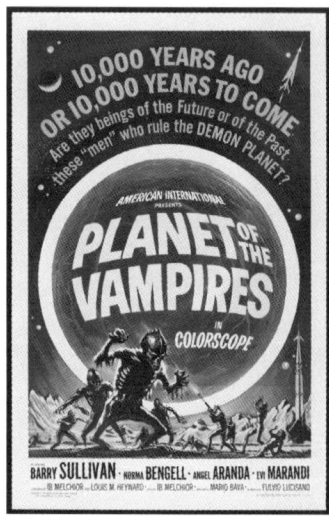

TWO TEAMS of astronauts respond to a distress signal on an eerie planet and discover a giant derelict spacecraft that houses the fossilized remains a giant alien race. The crew are infected by the parasitic aliens who, as it turns out, have intentionally lured them there. Sound familiar? Mario Bava's *Planet of the Vampires* (1965) was assuredly on Dan O'Bannon's mind when he wrote the screenplay for Ridley Scott's sci-fi/horror masterpiece *Alien* (1979). Scott may also have been subconsciously influenced by Bava's Technicolor sci-fi horror hybrid with its gothic, cavernous sets and spooky, fog-shrouded atmosphere.

The title is something of a misnomer, though, as there are no vampires to be found on planet Aura. Rather, the aliens are a breed of bodysnatching parasites that cause the death and reanimation of human bodies. (They are a dying race in need of a new home.) A more appropriate name would have been *"Planet of the Zombies."* But Bava's plastic-wrapped, leather-clad "vampires" and deft use of smoke and small spaces make this Samuel Z. Arkoff produced cheapie a must-see cult classic in the genre. And not forgetting the exquisite poster art.

THE SPANISH TRAGEDY

THOMAS KYD'S PROTOTYPICAL REVENGE TRAGEDY was one of the most popular plays of the Elizabethan and Jacobean periods. In it, Hieronimo seeks revenge for the murder of his son, who returns to the world of the living to watch the spectacle unfold alongside the character of Revenge. Practically every character in the play is brutally killed or commits suicide. The piece sparked a series of incredibly violent stage plays that focused specifically on murder and death over simple revenge, most notably Christopher Marlowe's *Tamburlaine* (1587), *Doctor Faustus* (1587-1589) and William Shakespeare's *Titus Andronicus* (1594), *Hamlet* (1600), and *Macbeth* (1605).

ANOTHER 10 HORROR MOVIE TAGLINES

1	*"It's not human, and it's got an axe!"* The Prey (1980)
2	*"Take the stairs. Take the stairs. For God's sake, take the stairs!!!"* The Lift (1983)
3	*"Please do not disturb Evelyn. She already is."* Mountaintop Motel Massacre (1986)
4	*"We are going to eat you!"* Zombie (1979)
5	*"A terrifying tale of sluts and bolts."* Frankenhooker (1990)
6	*"They're back from the grave and ready to party!"* The Return of the Living Dead (1985)
7	*"By pick, by axe, by sword, bye bye!"* The Mutilator (1985)
8	*"Ding, dong, you're dead."* House (1986)
9	*"If you have guts . . . HE WANTS THEM!"* Nightbeast (1982)
10	*"To avoid fainting, keep repeating 'It's only a movie . . . It's only a movie . . .'"* The Last House on the Left (1972)

JUMP SCARE

YOU KNOW IT WELL, it's that cheap horror film device in which the director racks up tension only to relieve it with a cat suddenly leaping out of a refrigerator, a hand landing on a shoulder or something equally stupid accompanied by an equally sudden sharp increase in musical pitch (AKA the "scare chord") and/or loud noise. Rarely used to advance the plot, the jump scare is nevertheless a regular horror movie trope. Other examples of overused tropes include the mirror scare; the trip and fall/twisted ankle drag; corpses that jump; the oversexed slut (first to die); the enlightened lunatic; the built on an Indian burial ground premise; "based on a true story;" Don't Go In The . . . basement, woods, attic, bathroom, garden, shed, barn; and finally; The End . . . or is it?

> *"[Horror] shows us that the control we believe we have is purely illusory, and that every moment we teeter on chaos and oblivion."*
> CLIVE BARKER (BORN 1952)
> *UK author, film director, screenwriter, producer, actor, playwright, artist*

THE THING

Among John Carpenter's most adored films, his masterpiece alien invasion film *The Thing* (1982) ranks second only to *Halloween*—but it didn't start out that way. Released just a few weeks after *E.T.*, *The Thing* was panned and otherwise unjustly maligned by critics and filmgoers alike. Rogert Ebert called it, "a grossout movie" that there was "no need to see" and *Newsweek* dubbed it, "atrocity for atrocity's sake." The negative reviews damaged Carpenter's career, but as the years would slowly reveal, *The Thing* was much more than the sum of its slimy, sentient parts.

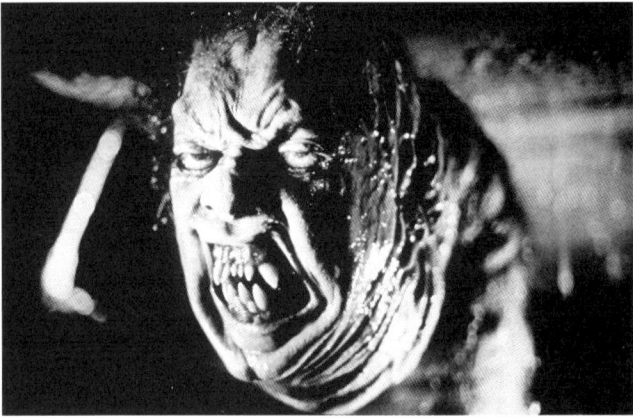

A spaceship crash lands on earth and is subsequently buried under Antarctic ice until discovered by Norwegian scientists who unwittingly thaw it out. When a mysterious dog is pursued into the camp of an all-male American research team by the aforementioned trigger happy Nords, a quiet apocalypse sets in as the creature begins to take on other forms, including humans. Upon its initial release, focus groups actually criticized the film for not having any female characters, which they felt meant there was no hope for the future. This ended up working in the film's favor.

Principal photography took place on a glacier near a mining town called Stewart, British Columbia, leaving the production at the mercy of the extreme weather. To be visually consistent, some scenes had to be completed over several days as they waited for the sun to disappear and snow to reappear. At one point the crew even got caught in a whiteout they barely made it out of, during a helicopter ride back to the glacier. Back in L.A., a 22-year-old special effects wunderkid named Rob Bottin, who had created jaw-dropping practical werewolves for Joe Dante's *The Howling* the previous year, was busy planning out the film's astonishing creature work and special effects sequences.

Despite the film's genius, people felt *The Thing* was too bleak and it nearly decimated Carpenter's career. He was subsequently fired from his next directing project, *Firestarter,* and was treated like an artistic failure known for doing pornographic violence. As hard as it was for the director to recover from *The Thing*, he did eventually move on to helm other films while his pariah of a movie slowly earned a cult following on video. Today *The Thing* is largely regarded among the best sci-fi horror films ever made. Many of its early detractors eventually took back all of the awful things they said about it upon its initial release.

AX WOUND

THE WORLD'S FIRST feminist horror publication, *Ax Wound* is a handmade zine lovingly curated by editor Hannah Neurotica, who also created the Ax Wound Film Festival and Women in Horror Recognition Month, which takes place each February. The zine's focus is the examination of "Gender in the Horror Genre" and its name is derived from a derogatory term for the menstruating vulva. In her mission statement Neurotica declares, "I want both the 'zine and the website to provide a safe, stimulating environment for feminist horror fans of all backgrounds to discuss the themes of gender, sexuality, and culture in the genre, both past and present."

Ax Wound also serves as a platform to help promote and bring together women working in the horror genre.

> "There are six ways a surgeon can cut the skull, and I figured Dr. Frankenstein, who was not a practicing surgeon, would take the easiest. That is, he would cut the top of the skull off straight across like a pot lid, hinge it, pop the brain in and clamp it tight. That's the reason I decided to make the monster's head square and flat like a box and dig that big scar across his forehead and have two metal clamps hold it together. The two metal studs that stick out the sides of the neck are inlets for electricity—plugs. Don't forget, the monster is an electrical gadget and lightning is his life force."
>
> JACK PIERCE (1889-1968),
> Universal's make-up artist on Frankenstein

THE BODY SNATCHERS

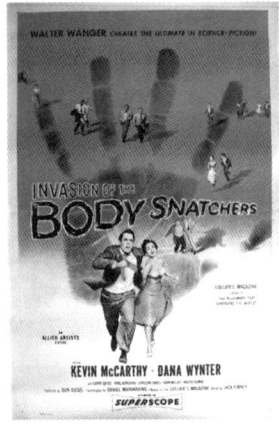

SEEDS DRIFT TO EARTH from outer space and begin replacing people with exact physical copies while they sleep. This is the premise of Jack Finney's 1955 alien invasion tale, *The Body Snatchers*. It's a deeply troubling, apocalyptic conceit, as the replacements have a five-year lifespan and cannot reproduce, which would leave the Earth completely devoid of human life if the invaders are not stopped. The book itself has an unsatisfying safe ending (for horror fans at least) in which the seeds retreat, but thankfully there are several film adaptations in which the bad guys win:

INVASION OF THE BODY SNATCHERS (1956) dir. Don Siegel
In a flashback, hysterical Dr. Miles Bennell recounts the story of how his town was invaded and overrun by pod people. The good doctors listening to his story eventually find out he is telling the truth in the director's uncharacteristically ambiguous ending for the Fifties.

INVASION OF THE BODY SNATCHERS (1978) dir. Philip Kaufman
This quiet apocalypse is by far the most masterful and disturbing version of Finney's tale. Few moments in cinema are as nerve-shatteringly terrifying as Donald Sutherland's ear-piercing shriek at the film's finale. One of the greatest paranoid thrillers ever made.

BODY SNATCHERS (1993) dir. Abel Ferrara
Snoozy remake of the 1978 film takes place on an army base with the central character a teenage girl. Using the military as a symbol of mindless conformity, Ferrara constructs a handful of paranoid scenes in this decent thriller, but can't seem to rise above a joyless and disingenuous script.

THE INVASION (2007) dir. Olivier Hirschbiegel and James McTeigue
The Invasion is basically a long car chase scene masquerading as a science fiction film. It has a few moments (the stranger banging on the front door), but lacks the subtlety at the heart of Finney's story, and fails as a psychological horror film.

THE TWILIGHT ZONE

ON OCTOBER 2, 1959, ROD SERLING's legendary anthology series *The Twilight Zone* premiered on American television to rave reviews. Though it wasn't the first of its kind, *The Twilight Zone* went on to become one of the best-known and most beloved anthology series in television history.

In 1958, Serling, a successful television writer, sold CBS a teleplay called *The Time Element*, which he hoped to produce as a weekly anthology series. Viewers loved it and the pilot—*Where is Everybody?*—was ordered in 1959. Serling wrote 92 of the show's 156 episodes, filling in the blanks with some huge names in horror at the time: Charles Beaumont, Ray Bradbury, Richard Matheson, and George Clayton Johnson all put pen to paper for *The Twilight Zone*.

Each episode was a self-contained drama with strong elements of science fiction and sometimes horror, often ending with an unexpected plot twist. Serling also starred as the show's host and narrator, using his closing monologue to explain how the episode's protagonist ended up in The Twilight Zone. The show ran for five seasons on CBS from 1959 to 1964. It has been revived twice, in 1985 and 2002.

THE MONKEY'S PAW

BE CAREFUL what you wish for. This is the moral of W.W. Jacobs' singular but significant contribution to the horror genre. In the story, the White family receives an allegedly magical monkey's paw with the power to grant three wishes, but the wishes are levied with a terrible tax on messing with fate. *The Monkey's Paw* (1902) is one of the most famous short horror stories ever written and has been adapted for screen many times (most notably with Bob Clark's *Deathdream*) as well as television, including *The Alfred Hitchcock Hour*, *The Twilight Zone*, and even *The Simpsons*.

ETYMOLOGY

THE WORD "HORROR" IS DERIVED from Middle English *horrour*, from Anglo-French **orur*, and directly from Latin; *L.horror*: "dread, veneration, religious awe," a figurative use, lit. "a shaking, trembling, shudder, chill," the action of bristling, from *horrēre* to bristle, shiver, "to bristle with fear, shudder,"; akin to Sanskrit *harṣate* "he shivers." First known use: 14TH century.

HALLOWEEN (1978)

DESPITE ITS MINISCULE BUDGET, John Carpenter's *Assault on Precinct 13* (1976) was a smash hit at film festivals across the globe. Among them, the Milan Film Festival, where it caught the attention of financier Moustapha Akkad and independent film producer Irwin Yablans, who acquired the film for American distribution. It performed poorly but didn't discourage Yablans and Moustapha from offering Carpenter a chance to write and direct a suspense film "about babysitters that are stalked and murdered by a psycho at night." Carpenter enlisted the help of then-girlfriend (and *Assault on Precinct 13* script supervisor) Debra Hill to write most of the female dialogue for a script called *The Babysitter Murders*, which would end up being retitled, *Halloween*.

The plot is superficially simple. On Halloween night in 1963, six-year-old Michael Myers (Will Sandin) inexplicably brutally murders his older sister Judith (Sandy Johnson) in the town of Haddonfield, Illinois (named after Carpenter's hometown in New Jersey). The boy is subsequently placed under the care of Dr. Loomis (Donald Pleasence) at Smith's Grove Sanitarium, where he remains in a catatonic state until his escape 15 years later, on October 30th. After stealing a car and Halloween mask, Myers returns to Haddonfield and begins stalking a teenager named Laurie Strode (Jamie Lee Curtis), who is babysitting two small children that evening. Myers murders her friends and relentlessly pursues her into increasingly claustrophobic settings until she is saved by the local sheriff along with Dr. Loomis, who has followed his patient to Haddonfield to stop him from killing again. Myers is shot and presumably killed, but vanishes at the end of the film, only to reappear in six sequels, a remake, and a sequel to the remake (Myers does not appear in *Halloween III: Season of the Witch*).

Akkad fronted $320,000 for the production, which took 21 days in South Pasadena, California. Carpenter received $10,000 for directing, writing, and composing the music, as well as retaining rights to 10% of the film's profits. Because of the film's low budget, Carpenter had to cut corners and hire crew in multitasking positions. Production designer/art director/location scout/co-editor/ Tommy Lee Wallace (who would later direct the third movie in the franchise) fashioned Michael Myers' iconic mask from a Captain Kirk mask purchased for $1.98. Some minor alterations including widening of the eyeholes and some bluish paint gave it the spooky, expressionless look that was indicated in the script.

The film was a massive hit and grossed $47 million at the US box office and over $60 million worldwide and was considered the most profitable independent film ever made, until *The Blair Witch Project* was released in 1999. It has been ruthlessly analyzed and celebrated by film critics and scholars as a benchmark North American slasher flick—a subgenre that takes inspiration from Michael

Powell's *Peeping Tom*, Alfred Hitchcock's *Psycho*, and the voyeuristic European gialli. Though it is often cited as the first North American slasher film, a similarly themed Canadian movie entitled *Black Christmas* (1974) predates *Halloween* by four years, and features a psycho killing college girls in their sorority house leaving one final girl—a theme that would later define the slasher subgenre.

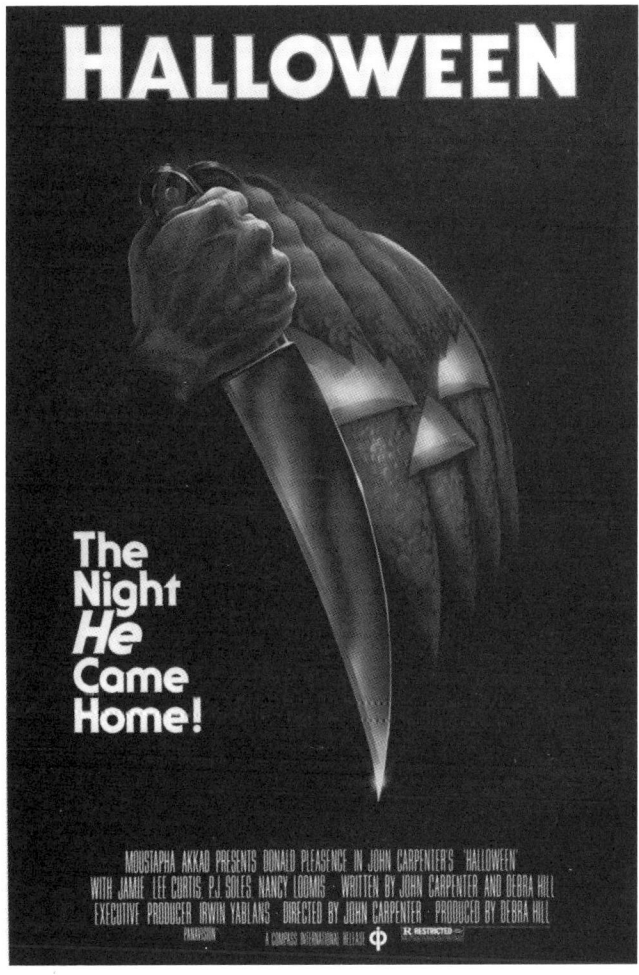

ANOTHER BODY COUNT BY HORROR MOVIE KILLERS

1	*Jack Frost* (1997)	66
2	Damien Thorn (*The Omen*, 1976)	62
3	*Predator* (1987)	57
4	*The Blob* (1958)	51
5	Horace Pinker (*Shocker*, 1989)	50
6	The "Its" (*It's Alive* series, 1974-2008)	45
7	Angela Baker (*Sleepaway Camp*, 1983)	45
8	*The Hidden* (1987)	42
9	The Outsiders (*Watchers* series, 1988-1994)	41
10	Johnny Bartlett (*The Frighteners*, 1996)	40

ROSEMARY'S BABY

BEING AN ADULT IS SCARY. There is immense pressure to succeed and multiply, and nowhere is this particular anxiety better represented than in Ira Levin's 1967 novel *Rosemary's Baby*. Rosemary Woodhouse wants to live in a nicer apartment and is willing to overlook the worst in her husband to make it happen. Guy, a vain, struggling actor, concocts a lie to get out of their current lease and the pair move into Bramford, a Gothic revival building with a history of witchcraft and murder. There they meet the Castevets, an elderly couple that Guy begins to spend a lot of time with. Guy's fortune turns around and he scores a role in a play when a theatre rival goes suddenly blind. He also announces he wants to have a baby with Rosemary following years of reluctance. After becoming mysteriously pregnant, Rosemary begins to suspect the Castevets are part of a Satanic coven who want to sacrifice her baby to the Devil. The truth, however, is much worse than Rosemary's worst fears.

Rosemary's Baby is on the surface a subtle religious horror tale with a Faustian bargain at its core. But more importantly, it is an early example of psychological horror, an introspective mode of the genre that builds on the paranoia of the 1950s (*Invasion of the Body Snatchers, The Thing from Another World*). Supernatural elements are downplayed in favor of Rosemary's interior hysteria. It is no surprise the book was a massive success in the 1960s, when social issues surrounding birth control and women's rights were at their peak. *Rosemary's Baby* was expertly adapted for cinema by Roman Polanski in 1968. Both the book and film represent psychological horror at its finest.

PEEPING TOM

RELEASED JUST MONTHS BEFORE PSYCHO, *Peeping Tom* is an uncompromising portrait of madness, sadoeroticism, and voyeurism that was tragically ahead of its time. The film was the subject of so much outrage and public consternation upon its initial release in Britain that it effectively decimated the career of its director, Michael Powell.

Peeping Tom stars Mark Lewis (played by Karlheinz Böhm), a serial killer who uses a film camera to document the expression of fear from his victims during their murders—making "snuff films" before the term had ever been invented. The film is also shot from the point of view of the killer, which implicates the audience in his disturbing crimes.

It was all too much for polite British filmgoers in 1960. The film opened to brutal reviews from critics, who accused it of being vulgar and perverse—which of course it was. People just weren't ready for *Peeping Tom* yet. Its killer was too sympathetic, too average, too much like the rest of us. It lasted just five days in theaters before being pulled and banned. Powell made one more film in Britain before retreating to Australia, his film career in ruins.

Peeping Tom quietly earned a cult following and was re-launched courtesy Martin Scorsese in America in the late-1970s, prompting a critical revaluation. Today it is considered a masterpiece of British cinema and is still consistently being reappraised. In the horror genre, it has had a tremendous stylistic influence on the voyeuristic Italian giallo and eventually, the American slasher film.

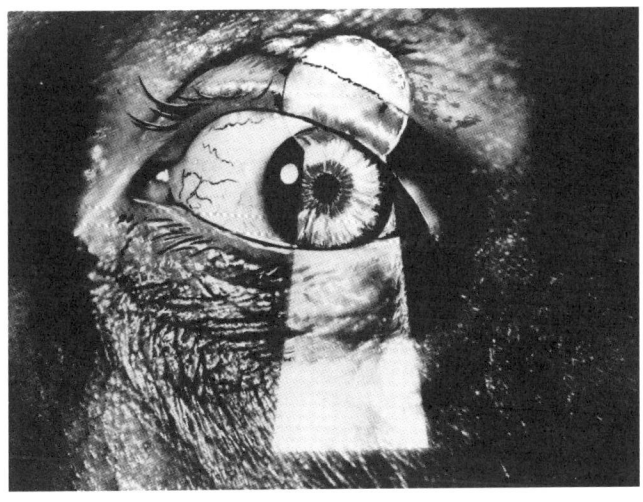

THE TEXAS CHAIN SAW MASSACRE

By now, everyone knows the story—a group of teenagers run afoul of a family of grave-robbing cannibals, The Sawyers, and a chainsaw wielding maniac living next to their grandpa's farmhouse. Sounds like the set up for a typical slasher film, but *The Texas Chain Saw Massacre* (1974) is much more than the sum of its parts.

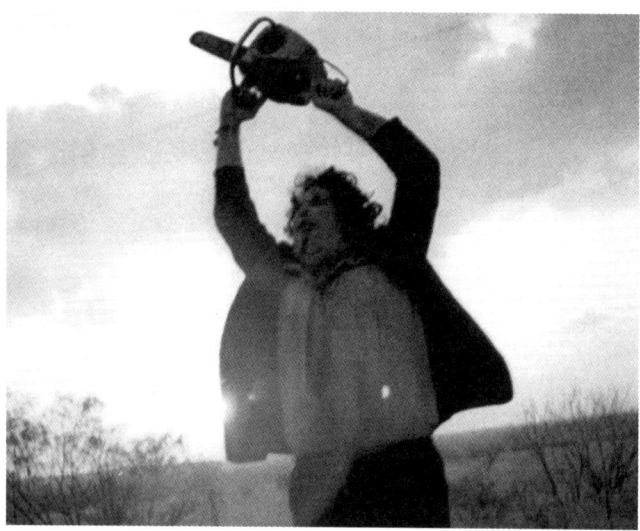

The opening of the film informs the audience that what they are about to see actually happened. It didn't, but that's part of the ruse. By this point in history the specter of Ed Gein still haunted the collective American subconscious. The country was in a state of decay and the film spoke directly to this growing anxiety about everything bad that was happening in post-'60s America—including the inconceivable crimes of Gein the grave robber, who lived in the farmhouse not too far away from the city. A film about a backwoods family terrorizing city kids could not have been more appropriate given the cultural zeitgeist.

The film's tagline asks, "Who will survive, and what will be left of them?" Setting up the template for future conventional slasher films, a final girl survives after much, much screaming and running—but the difference here is that she survives by sheer luck: She is saved by a passerby. The Sawyer family is not captured and social order is not restored. In spite of its bombastic title,

The Texas Chain Saw Massacre is more of a psychological horror film than the exploitive slasher it has often been misidentified as. It is in an important landmark in the progression of American independent cinema and a powerful film that commands further respect upon repeat viewings. Yes, it's a grueling experience, but that experience is shaped by aural violence, foreboding atmosphere, and manic intensity, rather than bloodshed. It is remembered for being excessively gory, but it's actually nearly bloodless. Think you saw that girl actually get hung on that meat hook? You didn't. Hooper just made you think you did using the power of suggestion.

THE VIDEO NASTIES

IN 1982 THE BRITISH DIRECTOR of Public Prosecutions successfully prosecuted and banned the films *Cannibal Holocaust* (1979), *Driller Killer* (1979), *I Spit on Your Grave* (1980), *Eaten Alive* (1980), and *SS Experiment Camp* (1976), for their violent content in England. This led to the Video Recordings Act 1984, which imposed bans or strict censorship on almost every horror film that made it into the country. Video shops were raided, rental tapes seized, and often charges were laid against retailers in possession of one of the 78 banned DPP titles. Film such as *The Texas Chain Saw Massacre* (1975) and *The New York Ripper* (1982) were banned in the UK and not released intact until 1999 and 2002, respectively—although *The New York Ripper* still has 29 seconds cut.

FRENCH DECADENCE

BORN IN PART OUT OF THE Gothic novel, especially the work of Edgar Allan Poe, the French Decadent movement was a brief but influential style of taboo-breaking late-19TH century *fin-de-siècle* French literature that included novels, poetry, and short fiction. The Decadents sought to "shock the middle class" with their work and espoused that art should exist for its own sake, independent of moral and social concerns. These stories celebrated decay—social and otherwise—and take pleasure in perversity as they explored themes of deviance—up to and including necrophilia. Decadent novelists include Charles Baudelaire (who translated Poe's work into French), Joris-Karl Huysmans, Theophile Gautier, and Octave Mirbeau. Prominent Decadent poets include Arthur Rimbaud, Auguste Villiers de l'Isle-Adam, and the Comte de Lautréamont. The English Decadents were 1890 figures such as Arthur Symons, Oscar Wilde, Ernest Dowson, and Lionel Johnson.

5 FINAL HORROR MOVIE TAGLINES

1	"You don't have to go to Texas for a chainsaw massacre." *Pieces* (1982)
2	"You can't wash away the terror." *The Washing Machine* (1993)
3	"Can a full-grown woman truly love a midget?" *Freaks* (1932)
4	"The only thing more terrifying than the last 12 minutes of this film are the first 92." *Suspiria* (1977)
5	"Sometimes dead is better." *Pet Sematary* (1989)

MALLEUS MALEFICARUM (1486)

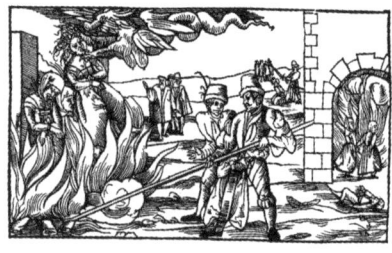

WRITTEN BY A GERMAN Catholic Clergyman named Heinrich Kramer, the *Malleus Maleficarum* (*The Hammer of Witches*) is an infamous treatise on the prosecution of witches during the Great European Witch Hunt. Its main purpose was to refute all arguments against the existence of witches, point out that witches were more often women than men (because women were weaker and therefore more susceptible to demonic temptations) and, of course, offer detailed explanation to magistrates on how to seek out, identify, and punish a witch. i.e. women who did not cry during their trial were automatically believed to be witches. In the text, Kramer accuses witches of infanticide, cannibalism, and even the extremely misogynistic power to steal penises. The very title of the book is feminine, implying right from the start that it is the women who are villains. The *Malleus Maleficarum* documents an unfortunate period on the historical record of ruthless sexism, rampant ignorance, and religious persecution of women as a result of the Reformation. It was condemned false by the Catholic Church in 1490, but continued to exert an influence until the Spanish Inquisition in 1538.

> "I played so many gentlemen in the beginning of my career that I wanted to play some villains and I got carried away."
> VINCENT PRICE (1911-1993), *US actor*

THEY CAME FROM WITHIN

SHIVERS, or, as it is known in Canada, *They Came From Within*, is the 1976 debut feature from David Cronenberg. But perhaps its working title best captures the theme of the film: *Orgy of the Blood Parasites* sees residents of an affluent high rise become infected with a sexually transmitted disease that turns them into sex-crazed maniacs. Cronenberg cut his teeth on this low budget picture that was (shockingly) partially financed with Canadian taxpayer money. Themes of body horror, transmogrification, and infection would come to define his cinematic work, including *Rabid* (1977), *The Brood* (1979), *Videodrome* (1983), *The Fly* (1986), *Dead Ringers* (1988), *Naked Lunch* (1991), and *eXistenZ* (1999). During this period he earned the nickname, "The King of Venereal Horror," though he wasn't particularly fond of the term.

DARIO ARGENTO

ITALIAN SCREENWRITER AND CRITIC Dario Argento made his directing debut in 1970 with the crime thriller, *The Bird with the Crystal Plumage*. Argento was inspired by Mario Bava's *Blood and Black Lace* (1964), but injected plenty of lurid imagery and heavy doses of eroticism resulting in a stylish, provocative giallo film. The world *giallo* is Italian for "yellow," referring to the Italian crime mystery pulp paperbacks of the day and their trademark yellow covers. Filmmakers such as Umberto Lenzi, Ernesto Gastaldi, Mario Bava, and even comedy director Lucio Fulci, began adapting these cheap novels to film in the 1960s, and soon the giallo became a genre of its own—characterized by operatic excess and plenty of sex and death.

Argento was pretty comfortable in this space and churned out two more gialli in what is referred to as his "animal trilogy": *The Cat o' Nine Tails* (1971), and *Four Flies on Grey Velvet* (1972), before hitting pay dirt with *Deep Red* (1975)—arguably one of the most well received and popular giallos ever made. By this time Argento was an international success and he branched out of giallo genre for *Suspiria* (1977), the arthouse supernatural technicolor spookshow for which he is most well known. *Suspiria* was succeeded by two sequels of diminishing quality: *Inferno* (1980), and *The Mother of Tears* (2007). Other Argento films of note include: *Tenebre* (1982), *Phenomena* (1985), *Opera* (1987), and *Trauma* (1993), *Masters of Horror*: "Jenifer" (2005). Though his more recent output—including 2012's *Dracula 3D*—shows a steady decline in quality, Argento's oeuvre has had a far-reaching impact on global horror cinema, most notably on the American slasher film.

INDEX

Ackerman, Forrest J. 24, 39
Akinari, Ueda 51
Alighieri, Dante 32
Argento, Dario 38, 42, 75, 93
Arkham House 24, 63
Ax Wound 83

"B" movies 10, 24
Barker, Clive 29, 43, 81
Báthory, Elizabeth 25
Bava, Mario 23, 76, 80, 93
Beaumont, Charles 85
Benchley, Peter 58
Bergman, Ingmar 62, 72
The Black Paintings 43
Black Sabbath 23
black-and-white films 72
Blair, Linda 74
The Blair Witch Project 65, 86
Bloch, Robert 37, 47, 50, 63
body counts 65, 88
The Body Snatchers 84
The Books of Blood 29
Bradbury, Ray 10, 24, 39, 50, 63, 85
Brooks, Louise 46
Brown, Frederic 27, 49
Byron, Lord 53, 55

Das Cabinet des Dr. Caligari 66
The Call of Cthulhu 41
Campbell, Eddie 46
Campbell Jr. John W. 54
Carpenter, John 11, 23, 30,
.... 53-54, 76, 78, 82-83, 86
The Castle of Otranto 13, 27
Castle, William 20, 60-61
Chambers, Robert W. 33, 70, 79
Chaney, Lon 6, 38, 52, 73
Chaney, Lon Jr. 6, 52
cinéma verité 62
Clover, Carol 36
Coffin Joe 79
Conrad, Joseph 42
Cooper, Alice 53
Cooper, Wyllis 44
Count Chocula 19
Craven, Wes 62, 75
Cronenberg, David 22, 44, 64, 93
Crowley, Aleister 23
Cunningham, Sean 64, 76

Danse Macabre 47, 63
Danzig, Glenn 71
De Luca, Michael 78
Decadent Movement 33, 91
Derleth, August 63
The Divine Comedy 32
Doctor Faustus 56, 80
Dr Jekyll and Mr Hyde 48-49
Dracula 6, 18-19, 22, 38, 46-47,
.... 53, 61-62, 67, 70, 73, 93
Du Maurier, Daphne 27

EC Comics 9
Edison Studios 64
The Exorcist 43, 74

Famous Monsters of Filmland ... 39, 71
Fifties films 10, 24
Final Girls 36, 87
Finney, Jack 84
Flynn, Gillian 57, 69
found-footage films 65
Frankenstein 6, 10, 12-13, 18, 31,
.... 43-44, 52, 55, 61-62, 64, 71, 73, 83
Freud, Sigmund 68
Friday the 13th 36, 43, 64, 75-76
Friedkin, William 74
From Hell 46
Fulci, Lucio 30, 42, 93
Furnier, Vincent 53
Fuseli, Henry 31

German Expressionism ... 66, 68, 73, 77
Ghost Stories of an Antiquary 58
Ghosts'n Goblins 69
Godzilla 10, 16-17, 41, 57
Goethe, Johann Wolfgang von 56
Golding, William 32
Goldwyn, Samuel 60
Gothic novels ... 13, 19, 27, 35, 40, 49,
.... 51, 70, 76, 91
Goya, Francisco 43
Grand Guignol 28, 53
Griffith, D.W. 75
Grimm's fairy tales 25

Halloween 36, 43, 76, 82, 86-87
Hammer Films 46, 61-62
Harryhausen, Ray 16
The Haunting of Hill House 26

Heart of Darkness 42
Hellboy 30, 57
Hitchcock, Alfred 37, 46-47, 64, 69, 85, 87
Hoffmann, E.T.A. 58, 68
Hugo, Victor 13, 38
The Hunchback of Notre Dame 6, 13, 35, 38, 73

I Am Legend 14, 20, 45
Impressionism 66
Inquisition 92
Interview with the Vampire 76
Ito, Junji 48

J-Horror 59
Jack the Ripper 18, 46, 77, 79
Jackson, Peter 39, 41, 64, 67
Jackson, Shirley 12, 26
Jacobs, W.W. 70, 85
James, Henry 70, 26
James, M.R. 58
Jaws 39, 58, 76
Johnson, George Clayton 85
jump scares 81

Kafka, Franz 15
Kammerspielfilm 66
Karloff, Boris 6-7, 20, 23, 34, 37, 39, 44, 47, 52, 73
King of Gimmicks 60
King Kong 16, 41, 57, 67
King, Stephen 9, 26, 29, 32, 36, 47, 73, 78
The King in Yellow 70, 79
Knock 49
Kyd, Thomas 80

Lang, Fritz 8, 66, 77
The Last House on the Left 62, 76, 81
Laughton, Charles 38, 72
Lewis, Herschell Gordon 48
Lights Out 44, 47
Lloyd's of London 60
Lord of the Flies 32
Lovecraft, H.P. 23, 30, 33-34, 41, 48, 50, 57, 63, 68, 78-79
Lugosi, Bela 6, 19, 73

M 8, 66
Machen, Arthur 23, 33
Malleus Maleficarum 92
La Manoir du Diable 44

Marchant, Guyot 63
Marins, José Mojica 79
Marlowe, Christopher 53, 56, 80
Matheson, Richard ... 14, 20, 45, 47, 85
matriarchs 64
Méliès, Georges 44
Metropolis 66
Misfits 71
Mondo Cane 65
The Monkey's Paw 70, 85
monsters 6, 10-11, 24, 39, 73
Moore, Alan 46

Nachtstücke 68
Nakata, Hideo 59
Naschy, Paul 18
Neurotica, Hannah 83
New Line Cinema 78
Night of the Living Dead 11, 14, 36, 45, 62, 71
Nightmare USA 35
Nosferatu 22, 66

Orgy of the Blood Parasites 93
Oscars 65, 74

Pan 23
Peeping Tom 37, 87, 89
penny dreadfuls 55
Perlman, Ron 57
Pierce, Jack 52, 83
Planet of the Vampires 80
Poe, Edgar Allan 13, 19-20, 24, 27-28, 31-33, 40, 59-60, 75, 91
Polanski, Roman 88
Polidori, John ... 12-13, 53, 55, 67, 72
Powell, Michael 37, 86-87, 89
Price, Vincent 14, 18, 20-21, 53, 92
Psycho 8, 37, 43, 64, 87, 89

Radcliffe, Ann 13, 27, 35
Radcliffe, Daniel 61
Rampo, Edogawa 19
Rice, Anne 76
Ringu 59
Romanticism 68
Romero, George 9, 11, 14, 22, 30, 36, 42-43, 45, 62, 65, 71, 75
Rosemary's Baby 60, 72, 88

The Sandman 68
Scorsese, Martin 89
sequels 43, 75

Shelley, Mary ... 12-13, 27, 31, 55, 64, 71
Shelley, Percy Bysshe ... 13, 55
shudder pulps ... 50
Smith, Dick ... 74
Stevenson, Robert Louis ... 48-49, 70
Stoker, Bram ... 19, 22, 27, 38, 47, 53, 67, 70, 73

taglines ... 51, 81, 92
Tales of Moonlight and Rain ... 51
The Texas Chain Saw Massacre ... 43, 51, 90-92
They Came From Within ... 93
The Thing ... 30, 51, 54, 78, 82-83
Thriller ... 11, 20, 47
Thrower, Stephen ... 35
The Trial ... 15
The Turn of the Screw ... 26, 70
The Twilight Zone ... 8, 69, 85

Universal ... 6, 10, 20, 52, 61, 66, 73, 83

vampires ... 14, 22, 45, 47, 53, 55, 62, 72, 76, 80
The Vampyre ... 12-13, 53, 67, 72
video games ... 11, 54, 57
Video Recordings Act ... 91

The Walking Dead ... 11
Walpole, Horace ... 13, 27
Wandrei, Donald ... 63
War of the Worlds ... 15, 24
Weird Tales ... 33, 41, 50
Welcome to My Nightmare ... 53
Welles, Orson ... 15, 60
Wells, H.G. ... 15, 20
Who Goes There ... 54
Wiene, Robert ... 66, 77
Wilde, Oscar ... 33, 70, 91
Wolgemut, Michael ... 63
The Woman in Black ... 61

zombies ... 9, 11, 14, 31, 36, 42, 45, 64, 69, 80-81

PICTURE CREDITS

All images are copyright their respective copyright holders and are shown here for historical and review purposes. Every effort has been made to credit the copyright holders, artists and/or studios/publishers whose work has been reproduced in these pages. We apologise for any omissions, which will be corrected in future editions, but must hereby disclaim any liability.

Plan 9 From Outer Space © 1959 Reynolds Pictures *p10* / *The Walking Dead* © 2011 Robert Kirkman *p11* / The Kobal Collection *p15* / RKO/The Kobal Collection *p16* / Toho/The Kobal Collection *p17* / Amachi Films/Aconito Films/The Kobal Collection *p18* / *Tales Of Terror* © 1962 Alta Vista Productions *p21* / Prana-Film/The Kobal Collection *p22* / MGM/The Kobal Collection *p26* / The Art Archive/Detroit Institute Of Arts/Superstock *p31* / Laurel Entertainment/The Kobal Collection *p36* / Independent International/The Kobal Collection *p39* / *Zombie* © 1978 Variety Film Productions *p42* / Courtesy Robert L. Lucas. *Night Of The Living Dead* © 1968 Image Ten *p45* / *Weird Tales*, March 1940, Popular Fiction Publishing Co. C Coll. Maison S'ailleurs/Agence Martienne *p50* / Universal/The Kobal Collection *p52* / Columbia/The Kobal Collection *p60* / Edison/The Kobal Collection *p64* / Wingnut Films/The Kobal Collection *p67* / *The Mummy* © 1931 Universal Pictures *p7, 70, 73* / Warner Bros/The Kobal Collection *p74* / Paramount/The Kobal Collection *p76* / Iberia Filmes/The Kobal Collection *p79* / *Planet Of The Vampires* © 1965 Aip/Castilla Cooperativa Cinematografica *p80* / Universal/The Kobal Collection *p82* / *Invasion Of The Body Snatchers* © 1956 Walter Wanger Productions *p84* / Falcon International/The Kobal Collection *p87* / Anglo Amalgamated/The Kobal Collection *p89* / Vortex-Henkel-Hooper/Bryanston/The Kobal Collection *p90*

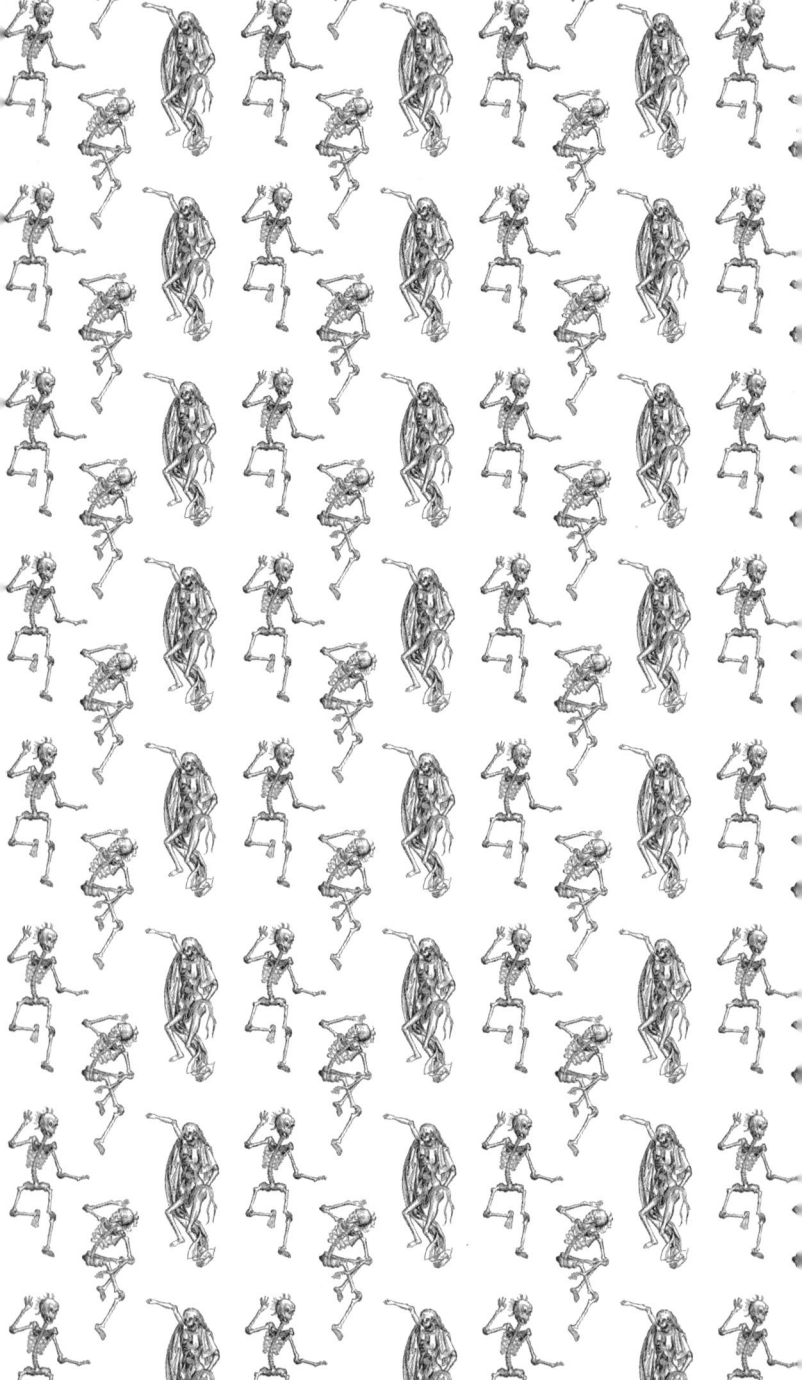